HANDBOOK
FOR
SHAKTIPĀT SIDDHA YOGA
INITIATES

HANDBOOK
FOR
SHAKTIPĀT SIDDHA YOGA
INITIATES

JAN ESMANN

Published by Blue Pearl Publications 2017
Roennebaervej 11, 2.tv., 2400 Copenhagen NV, Denmark

2. edition 2017

ISBN-13: 9781541281677
ISBN-10: 541281675

Printed by CreateSpace

Editing: Lila Sterling
Cover design: Sandra York
Layout: Laura Jenkins

The author's email: jan@lovebliss.eu

Other books by Jan Esmann

On spirituality:

Lovebliss – the Essence of Self-realization

Enlightenment 101 – From Ignorance to Grace

Kundalini Tantra – Song of Liberation

On the materials and methods of the artist:

The Artist's Craft – A Handbook

On art history:

Figurative Art of the 21st Century

Short stories (In Danish)

Strandvaskeren

Table of Contents

Mother's Grace

Everything on this path comes from the grace of Mother Divine.

It also comes from Krishna, the Divine Blue Being who initiated me into this path back in March of 1979.

The grace of these two Divinities is beyond description, it is beyond human comprehension, it has to be experienced.

Krishna is capricious and playful.

Mother will always be there for you. Always.

Basics of
Shaktipāt Siddha Yoga

INTRODUCTION

Shaktipāt initiation grants you the grace of an automatic sādhana (spiritual practice and path) known as Shaktipāt Siddha Yoga. Other traditions give it other names: Siddha Yoga (Perfect Yoga) and Kundalinī Mahā Yoga (the Greatest Yoga of the Awakened Kundalinī). Rather than you reaching out to the Self, the Self now reaches out to you. This is grace and is the hallmark of shaktipāt, no matter what shaktipāt lineage you are initiated into. It has to be given to you by an enlightened Siddha. It is also perfect because all other yoga lineages are naturally and automatically fulfilled through the grace of the Divine Mother, Shakti. You cannot learn Siddha Yoga by study or get it through your own effort. Once you have received shaktipāt and your kundalinī has become active, you are a Siddha Yogi; a follower of the Siddha path. The word 'yoga' means 'union' and designates both the path to union as well as the state of union. A 'yogi' is one who pursues this goal of union with the Self. Once you have been initiated and become a Siddha yogi, no matter what practice you engage in, even if you decide to give up the practices suggested in this book, you will still be a Siddha Yogi as long as your main practice is to invoke, awaken and surrender to the Divine Mother: Shakti. Your inner guru.

Undoubtedly, all spiritual paths aim at this awakening of kundalinī, but they all require arduous effort over a long period of time. With shaktipāt the enlightened Siddha guru awakens it for you. The guru may also impart a glimpse or experience of samādhi, which will guide you in your future sādhana and inspire you.

INITIATION

All the student can and should do during personal initiation is to let go and remain open. When receiving shaktipāt *in absentia*, the student should meditate doing Kundalinī Kriyā or Kriyā Prānāyāma.

Mālās (rosaries) and other blessed objects

If you have received shaktipāt in absentia
In the envelope mailed to you, there is a rudraksha mālā (rosary of rudraksha seeds); this mālā carries the shaktipāt energy. Wear it during meditation only. Wear it under your shirt so it touches the skin. Don't let anybody else touch the mālā. If you have also received fruit or candy apart from the mālā, eat it just before sitting for your first meditation. Don't give it to somebody else.

Upon initiation

If you are initiated *in absentia* please wear the mālā every time you meditate (under your shirt so it touches the skin). Do not share it with anyone else. If they accidentally touch it, no problem. But it is meant for you and you alone. Meditate to the guided Kundalinī Kriyā Meditation. Meditate diligently for at least ten days with the mālā (upon receiving it). After the ten days pick any of the given meditations you prefer. During the ten days: no pot/hash/mushrooms/ayahuasca/San Pedro/drugs/etc. Don't get drunk and preferably no sex during the ten-day period. This goes both for *in absentia* initiations as well as personal initiations.

After shaktipāt initiation

Following shaktipāt initiation, meditate (at least) twice daily for ten days. This is very important! Don't skip a day during the ten-day initiation process.

If you are receiving shaktipāt at a three day shaktipāt intensive, you will know the techniques well after the three days and will not need the CD (or mp3), but you can use them if you like.

Krishna and Devi Shaktipāt

These initiations are only given in person during an intensive. During shaktipāt another thing takes place: A seed, or imprint, of enlightenment is planted deep within you, this is called Shivapāt, and this will come to fruition eventually and grant you liberation (*mukti*). It is impossible to say in general when this happens, but if you meditate daily and make a practice out of sensing the Shakti in you and surrendering to it as best you can throughout the day, you have done your part and the Shakti will do the rest. Mother will guide you.

Shaktipāt during intensives

When you receive shaktipāt during an intensive, you will not receive or need a mālā. However, you can bring your own mālā to the intensive since Jan usually infuses mālās in the evening of the first day. Remember to tag it with your name (important). Rudraksha mālās are usually for sale at the intensive.

Daily meditation after shaktipāt

Keep meditating every day after the ten days. The full Kundalinī Kriyā meditation lasts 50 minutes. I know for some it may be hard to find time for two 50 minute meditations, like if you have a job and children. If this is the case, at least meditate once every day, or meditate two times for 25 minutes.

Shaktipāt will connect you with divine grace. Meditation is the way to get that grace flowing. Shaktipāt without meditation is not enough, neither is meditation without shaktipāt. It is like gasoline (Shakti) and a car (meditation). The car needs gasoline to work, and gasoline without a car won't take you anywhere. Similarly, meditation without Shakti is dry and slow and like fumbling in the dark in fruitless attempts to reach the Self. If you have received shaktipāt and don't invite the awakened energy (kundalinī Shakti) to work in you, which is what you do when meditating, you won't get far.

Remember the important thing is not so much to do the meditation practices well or 'correctly', as it is to <u>surrender to the particular sense of Shakti (the spiritual energy of the Self) that arises within you</u>.

SHAKTIPĀT

Shaktipāt is a very sacred and very rare initiation. Shaktipāt means a transference of Shakti (the spiritual energy of the Self) from the master to the student with the aim of awakening the otherwise dormant kundalinī in the student, so that the kundalinī Shakti (divine energy) begins to work for his enlightenment. It is possible to change the behavior of kundalinī so that kundalinī, instead of upholding your ignorance begins to deconstruct it and change your nervous system so that you can uphold states of enlightenment. This change in kundalinī is really what all spiritual paths aim at, but very few succeed. The fastest and most direct path to it is known as shaktipāt. Shaktipāt simply means that an enlightened Siddha, who has completed the kundalinī process, instigates this process towards enlightenment in the student. This instigation is all that shaktipāt is about.

Shaktipāt can be given in a number of ways: By touch, look, or thought; via an object (such as a mālā); via a fruit or other edible substance. There are probably other ways, but these are the ones I use.

Does the guru lose his energy when giving shaktipāt?

No, not really. This depends on his level of enlightenment, of course. But a fully realized and adept Siddha guru does not lose his energy. He is merely a conduit for the grace of the Divine Mother. He may pick up some of the student's karma, though, and this can be temporarily unpleasant for the guru. It is important that the student, when approaching the guru for shaktipāt, does not have any agendas such as 'take my pain', 'solve my problems' and so on, as such will certainly dump the bad karma on the guru and cause him unnecessary suffering.

Levels of shaktipāt

When giving shaktipāt, it differs from person to person what they receive. Shaktipāt also differs from guru to guru. The differences depend on the student's ability to receive, the student's level of spiritual evolution, the guru's level of enlightenment and the guru's ability to give shaktipāt. In general, we can speak of the following kinds of shaktipāt:

A. Shaktipāt for enlightenment

1. Instant enlightenment.

2. Enlightenment within a very short time (a few weeks or at most months).

B. Shaktipāt for kundalinī awakening that ensures:

1. Enlightenment in this lifetime.

2. Instant access to the deepest samādhi. Sat-Chit-Ānanda.

3. Access to the deepest samādhi within this lifetime.

4. Enlightenment within a few lifetimes.

5. The student will continue on the path of Shaktipāt Siddha Yoga in the next life.

C. Shaktipāt that prepares for higher forms of shaktipāt

1. Untying one or more of the knots (granthis).

2. Cleaning energy channels, in particular Sushumnā.

Other situations that involve a master and a client should be mentioned, since they have nothing to do with shaktipāt, yet some call them so. These are of no value with respect to getting enlightened. These are the lowest forms of deliberate energy interaction between two or more people (unfortunately many have begun calling them shaktipāt):

1. Healing
2. Energy work

Only an enlightened guru can give shaktipāt for enlightenment and for kundalinī awakening (A and B). Some such gurus may initiate non-enlightened students to give the 'C' kinds of shaktipāt that cleanse the system and prepare it for the higher forms of shaktipāt.

What Shaktipāt Isn't

There are many misconceptions about what shaktipāt is. The following passage by swami Satyānanda contains most of them, so let's discuss it:

> "The ninth method of awakening [kundalinī] is performed by the guru. It is called shaktipāt. The awakening is instant, but it is only a glimpse, not a permanent event. When the guru creates this awakening you experience samādhi. You can practice all forms of prānāyāma and all āsanas, mudrās and bandhas without having learned them or prepared for them. All the mantras are revealed to you and you know the scriptures from within. Changes take place in the physical body in an instant. The skin becomes very soft, the eyes glow and the body emits a particular aroma which is neither agreeable nor disagreeable."
> (Satyānanda Saraswati, Swami: Kundalinī Tantra, Yoga Publications Trust, Bihar, India, 2001 (1984), p.48.)

The awakening is instant, but it is only a glimpse, not a permanent event.

When a competent, enlightened Siddha yogi awakens the student's kundalinī through shaktipāt it is most certainly permanent. Thus, it is not an 'event', but a radical shift in how kundalinī operates. The kundalinī will remain awake for at least three incarnations and in those inspire the student to do sādhana (spiritual practices for attaining enlightenment) and receive shaktipāt again. If the student does not follow-up on the shaktipāt initiation by doing spiritual practices, the kundalinī will become restful, but not dormant. This means that if the lazy student picks up sādhana at a later stage, the kundalinī is ready to become active and arise and will inspire the student to receive another shaktipāt initiation.

When the guru creates this awakening you experience samādhi

Some do, some don't. It is highly individual. Some go into such a deep samādhi, they become nonfunctional and can hardly move. Some faint. Some don't experience a thing, but their kundalinī is nevertheless influenced to some degree, though it may not be entirely awakened. Then again, some experience nothing during the shaktipāt initiation, but when they go home and meditate regularly, they suddenly feel heat rising in the spine, which is a classic shaktipāt symptom.

[When the guru creates this awakening,] you can practice all forms of prānāyāma and all āsanas, mudrās and bandhas without having learned them or prepared for them.

This is a complete misunderstanding of how shaktipāt works. When you receive shaktipāt, you do not spontaneously become agile and knowledgeable of all sorts of esoteric yogic practices. But what may happen as the kundalinī, which has been awakened through shaktipāt, operates in you is that the body may spontaneously adopt various postures and movements and some of these do conform to some of the mentioned yogic practices. But most of them don't! These spontaneous movements and postures are called 'kriyās' and they should be allowed to happen unless one is meditating in a public place, of course.

[When the guru creates this awakening,] all the mantras are revealed to you and you know the scriptures from within.

You do not suddenly know all the Tantric and yogic mantras! Nor all the scriptures! But what does happen in due course is that as kundalinī grants you enlightenment, you realize the meaning of all the scriptures about enlightenment without having studied them.

9

Of course you do; you are enlightened and the scriptures are about enlightenment, but since you are already enlightened, you have no need for the scriptures.

[When the guru creates this awakening,] changes take place in the physical body in an instant. The skin becomes very soft, the eyes glow and the body emits a particular aroma which is neither agreeable nor disagreeable.

This statement is so bizarre, I can't even comment on it. But yes, if the student enters samādhi and is filled with bliss, of course the eyes glow!

KUNDALINĪ

Kundalinī is the most important thing on our path. Initially you will experience kundalinī as a separate energy apart from you that is operating in the body and nervous system. Later you will realize that this Shakti of kundalinī emanates from the Self and as it develops you will realize it is the grace of the Divine Mother working in you for your enlightenment and liberation. Eventually you will realize it is the Self, yet you will overflow with devotion for Mother.

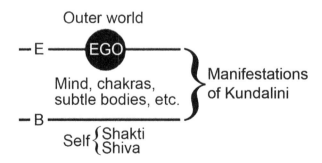

First we have to understand that the absolute Self (below the line 'B' in the diagram) is one's innermost pure being (as distinct from the small self, the ego), and understand that it is utterly unmanifest – yet it has two 'qualities': in-itself-resting-pure-being (called *Shiva*), and dynamic creative potential (called *Shakti*). Shiva and Shakti are one and the same, but for convenience sake we talk of two principles. They can be realized separately or in and as their natural oneness. Other sādhanas but Shaktipāt Siddha Yoga usually first realize the void (Shiva). Most stop there and think it is the end-all, because what could be higher than the unmanifest (they ask). They are so wrong; that is just the beginning. Shaktipāt Siddha Yoga gives you both Shakti and Shiva together in one package; both the void and the bliss at once.

In the diagram above, imagine you are the pure state of oneness with the Self, which is your natural state. There is, in that state, nothing above the lower line 'B' (for *Bindu*), even Bindu is not there. The first thing that happens when the Self decides to manifest as an individual entity, is that Shakti contracts into a point (called *Bindu*) and this Bindu is the origin-point of kundalinī; nay, it is the essence of kundalinī. For ultimate liberation to happen, this point has to collapse back into the Self. Kundalinī then, in its process of manifesting you as an ignorant entity, manifests everything between 'B' and 'E', which means you as an ignorant individual on all levels of existence. Kundalinī then goes into a state of 'sleep' an inch or so above the root chakra in a place called *kanda*. In fact, it does not sleep. It is continuously active in upholding your structure of ignorance, your psyche, mind, subtle bodies, and so on; everything that is ignorant-you is a manifestation of this sleeping kundalinī. However, there is very little spiritual progress towards enlightenment, there is just change within the status quo of ignorance and most ignorant people believe this change within the status quo is spiritual progress. It is not. It is merely ego change towards a (hopefully) nicer ego and it will never lead to enlightenment, though that is usually what these deluded souls imagine and dream it is all about. Enlightenment does not give you a Christ-like personality or ego, it makes you free, gives you ultimate freedom. Do you really understand the implications of that one word? Free!

Since the entire structure of you is and has been manifested by kundalinī, kundalinī has within itself a 'blueprint' of that structure. Kundalinī, therefore contains within itself the necessary knowledge to intelligently reconstruct that structure so you can uphold states of enlightenment.

Symptoms of an awakened kundalinī during meditation

Supreme bliss.

Supreme love.

Supreme devotion.

Crying.

Laughing.

Heat in the lower part of the spine.

Heat in the entire spine.

Heat and/or tingling in the hands and/or feet.

Cold energy in the body and/or spine.

Tingling on the skin like small insects crawling.

Sensation of being caressed with a feather on the inside of the skin.

Brilliant white light in the head.

Energy in the brain.

Pressure inside the head.

Energy pressure in any of the chakras.

Sensation of a needle piercing the body at a chakra location.

Sensation of energy being sucked out of the genitals and pulled into the spine.

Spontaneous body or limb movements.

Body arching backwards.

Head arching backwards.

Spontaneous mudrās or bandhas.

Uttering more or less meaningful words and phrases spontaneously.

Speaking gibberish spontaneously.

Kriyās and experiences

During meditation, you may initially feel the Shakti as tingling in the hands and face or the feet; as a pressure at the top of the head or as heat in the perineum or spine. The body may perform spontaneous movements (kriyās) like twitching the spine, shaking the limbs, rapid breathing or even uttering meaningless words. Do not be alarmed by any of this but sink into it and let it happen. Also, ecstasies may arise where the eyelids flicker and the mind races with thoughts and you are very blissful. Also, this is a good sign so let it happen. Do not fight or resist any of these experiences as they are all good signs that the Shakti is grabbing you and working in you. Later you may have a feeling that it is not you that is meditating on the Self, but rather the Self that is meditating on you and you can't do anything but surrender to divine grace. This is very good and is, indeed, what is actually going on.

Sādhana with or without kundalinī

There are many kinds of spiritual practice (sādhana), some are like walking to a given destination, some are like driving there in a car. One is very slow, the other is very fast. The slow one, walking, does not require any fuel; the fast one, the car, needs fuel. The fuel of the fast sādhana is kundalinī. Once that is said, you have to understand that you need both the car and the fuel. A car with no fuel will take you nowhere; a canister of fuel will in itself take you nowhere. Similarly, kundalinī, without regular sādhana will not take you far. In some advanced cases it seems like kundalinī is doing everything for a person, while the person does not do any sādhana. This is only appearance. In reality such a person is living sādhana all the time and does therefore not sit and meditate regularly, or do other practices; there is no need for them. The person lives sādhana. Needless to say, such students are quite advanced.

Arousal of an un-awakened (sleeping) kundalinī

People who have not received shaktipāt, yet meditate, can sometimes experience a lot of unexpected energy being released from the root chakra into the body. It may even be the kundalinī shakti temporarily rising. This has nothing to do with an awakening, though it is often called that. It is an *arousal* and it is temporary and has very little benefit for their spiritual progress, unless they harness it and channel it through various rigorous kriyās (a set of āsanas, concentrations, mudrās, bandhas, prānāyāmas and so on to be performed for a few hours every day without fail). They usually never want to do this. Negative kundalinī arousals sometimes happen to people who are doing wrong meditation practices. I once met a lady who complained to me of her unpleasant kundalinī situation. After questioning her a while she explained how she had been meditating for years: She would visualize the kundalinī leaving the root chakra and pass out of her body behind her back, there she would visualize it moving in a circular motion outside the body up above the head and enter the head through the third eye. No wonder she had terrible kundalinī problems! And she still blamed kundalinī for her problems and not her irresponsible meditation practice. I tried, kindly, to explain this to her, but she would not listen and would not try my meditation nor receive shaktipāt. She just expected me to make her kundalinī go away. Of course, such is not possible.

A kundalinī awakening through shaktipāt initiation by a Siddha is entirely benign and it has an intelligence within it that knows what to do when and how much you can handle. It might push you to the limit, but it never crosses the line. Mother's grace is running the show.

THE SELF AND THE SELF

You have to distinguish between the small self (small s) and the absolute Self (capital S). The absolute Self, or the Self for short, is the real You. It is entirely unmanifest, yet its nature is pure being, consciousness and bliss (sat-chit-ānanda). It is also known as pure being and creative, dynamic potential (Shiva and Shakti). The small self, which you identify with, is not you. It is a construct. Though the small self is real enough as a psychic energy phenomenon, the sense that it is you is an illusion. Getting enlightened means freeing yourself of the illusory sense of yourself and merging back into the absolute Self. There is nothing wrong or bad about the small self. You could not function in the world without it. The problem is you erroneously assume it is you.

The small self is a manifestation of kundalinī shakti. Kundalinī is the primal contraction of the Shakti of the absolute Self. The small self is there as a vehicle through which to act in and interact with the world. Actually, the absolute Self does not identify with the small self, though I said in the previous paragraph you identify with it. The real You is of course the Self.

What is going on is that the mind, the small self, is compartmentalized and constructed out of all sort of bits and pieces. These billions of pieces are past impressions, experiences, thoughts, emotions and so on, as well as present ones. In the following diagram, these are represented by the circles with the letters in them.

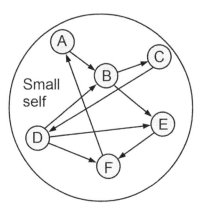

What happens is that part A harbors the notion that it is B; B harbors the notion that it is C and E; C that it is D; D that it is B, E and F; and so on. For example, a man wears a certain aftershave; he does so because part of him, perhaps his sense of sex-appeal, identifies with past impressions concerning that aftershave. These can be numerous: Someone he admired used it; an advertisement made an impression; and so on. All this adds up to an identity network within the psyche. The point of this is to illustrate that it is an unfathomably complex network of identifications that add up to the identity which constitutes the small self. It should also illustrate that it is a fiction. Believing this fiction is You is the definition of *ignorance*.

Consciousness is not produced by these networks. The individual elements, A, B, C and so on, are lifeless contractions within the psyche. Consciousness is invested into this complex network and the combination constitutes the entity of the small self. The goal of the yogi is to realize the nature and source of this consciousness and his sādhana is nothing but an investigation into this. In other words, the consciousness becomes aware of itself as independent of the contractions making up the small self, and this consciousness wants to realize its own very nature.

The research of the yogis, past and present, reveal that consciousness (or 'awareness' or whatever you want to call it) is in its essential nature unmanifest, but it can contract into the various identity-structures of the small self. Normally the word 'consciousness' refers to the state of being aware of something, thus consciousness seems to be tied up with the relative world and phenomena, physical or psychic or otherwise. But when consciousness is thoroughly explored, one realizes that it is, in its essential nature, unmanifest. This has a couple of ramifications. First, it means that there is no difference between pure being and consciousness. Second, it means that pure being can be conscious of itself without ceasing to be unmanifest. This self-consciousness of pure, unmanifest being, in its fullest extent, is Self-realization. This is the first goal of the yogic exploration. It is the first state of enlightenment. It is liberation.

A catch-phrase that can be used about the unmanifest is *non-duality*. It is a stupid phrase much in misuse today. Since it refers to the unmanifest, it is a misleading phrase, for there isn't even room for a negation in what is unmanifest. The unmanifest Self simply IS. This does not mean the phrase 'I AM' describes it any better, since there is no 'I' in what is unmanifest.

The next question that arises is this: *Since my very Self is unmanifest and your very Self is unmanifest are they not one and the same?* This question has troubled seekers since time immemorial. The naïve and simplistic answer is that they are indeed the same and that there is only one Self. It is naïve because the question and the subject of the question lie in separate paradigms or dimensions. The paradigm of the subject invalidates the paradigm of both the question and its possible reply, since the reply lies within the paradigm of the question. So, the answer to the question is 'No'. Once enlightened, one realizes that though each Self is unmanifest, all Selves remain individual and unique. In fact, Patanjali, who systematized Yoga, in his famous *Yoga Sūtras* states that God is a special soul distinct from other souls, thus implying that even though the Self is unmanifest, Selves are unique and individual. This is not, and I stress *not*, teaching duality. The problem is that language fails. When enlightened you can make two contradicting statements about the Self that both are true:

1. There is only One infinite ocean of Being which is bliss and love and I am That.
2. You are that too, let's enjoy it together.

This 'enjoy it together' implies separation within the Oneness. The first statement implies there is no such separation. The two statements are incompatible, yet both are true. This is because language fails.

The Self is infinite, unmanifest bliss, love, joy and devotion to God. When enlightened, you see God in everything and your heart melts in devotion and love. God has many forms. On our path, the Divine Mother and Krishna are particularly important. The Divine Mother is Shakti; She lives within you as kundalinī. Initially kundalinī seems to be some strange energy inside the body. Eventually one realizes that kundalinī and Shakti are One and are one with the Self. Here we have another paradox that arises because language fails. Know that Mother is all; She is the Mother of Devotion; She is the object of devotion. Everything is BLISS.

THE GURU

A guru is a spiritual teacher. The word 'guru' means one who takes you from darkness 'gu' to light 'ru'. It also means one who has traversed that path from ignorance to enlightenment, though far from all gurus are enlightened. Thus, there are as many gurus as there are paths. When you pick a guru, he should at least be enlightened, but that is not enough on our path. On our path, the guru should be enlightened and also have completed the kundalinī process to its very end where kundalinī merges back into Shiva/The Void in the brain. Such a guru should furthermore be appointed by Mother or the Blue Being to initiate others into our path of shaktipāt. Such a guru can, furthermore, on behalf of Krishna or Mother, initiate others into teaching. But mahādiksha (the greatest initiation by God) is only given by the Blue Being or Mother. Mother can give it through the guru, of course. Mahādiksha is a rare event.

The guru is not necessarily a saint. He can be a normal person with a family. He can have flaws like smoking, drinking or swearing, or be angry like U. G. Krishnamurti (*UG*). It is unlikely, though, that a true guru could be a pervert or an erotomaniac, since the sexual energy in the real guru will most likely be transmuted into spiritual energy. Some great gurus, like Nisargadatta, smoked; he even owned a tobacco store. Usually ignorant people, especially those influenced by the New Age religion's preachers, think that to be enlightened is to be pure and like Christ.

A saint is not necessarily enlightened. He or she is a person who has perfected the character and lifestyle to a very high degree. Mother Theresa of Calcutta was a saint, but she was not enlightened as can be surmised from her letters. Sometimes enlightened beings are saints, like Mata Amritānandamayi Devi (*hugging Amma*) or the late Ānandamoyi Ma or Shri Ramakrishna.

You do not become a guru just because you are initiated into sannyās (swami monkhood) and wear orange clothes, or are initiated into brahmācharya (a swami aspirant living in celibacy) and wear white clothes. Outer appearances do not matter at all. In fact, there is a special title or name for enlightened beings who do not follow the common order of things. Such a person is called an *Avadhoota*. They are considered strange because they go their own way and do things their own way. Most enlightened beings are strange and unpredictable to some extent, but Avadhootas are beyond rules and common or traditional practice. Such beings are also often called Siddhas, which means a perfected being. A Siddha is not perfect in the traditional moral or ethical sense of proper conduct. He is perfected within, and his life is a spontaneous expression of his inner state of enlightenment. Some Avadhootas and Siddhas dress strangely or have strange matted hair, others you would not recognize on the street.

A real guru is radiant. Not all the time, but when he meditates or dives within or otherwise opens up the sluices to his connection with Mother Divine. When you meditate with a real guru, you become suffused with peace and sometimes bliss and love for God. Someone who has merely learned to think and talk non-duality is not a guru at all; in fact, he is a fraud misguiding sincere seekers. The world is full of such fools today.

You need a living guru, but students are afraid of having living gurus; they prefer dead gurus who will not contradict them and tell them if their ideas and directions in spirituality are wrong. They feel more safe having a dead guru; of course, an inaccessible living guru is just as good. People who pick such gurus just want someone they can admire or worship and dream about, and in doing so can boost their egos into believing they are good disciples of the greatest master – and thus *really spiritual* and *elect* – the more famous the guru, the better. Most disciples of inaccessible famous gurus want to feel elect. It is the same with many Buddhists; they usually take subtle pride in being Buddhists and subtly feel spiritually better than others.

The real guru loves his students, no matter how he treats them. All he wants is for them to become enlightened, become liberated. He wants them to live in bliss. Some he will be kind and loving towards, others he will scold and be angry with. To the guru, it is all the same. Students may get shocked and annoyed if they see the guru scold somebody, or ask them to either change or leave the *sangha* (spiritual community under the guru). They don't understand that the guru is trying to help that person awaken by confronting them with their ignorance and asking them to choose between that and grace. In reality a true guru is full of love and devotion to Mother within each and every one. He sees the Supreme Self in everybody and it hurts the guru to see people cling to their ignorance – especially if they do so in the name of spirituality, which is often the case.

Choosing a guru

This is a serious matter and should not be taken lightly. A guru should fit the disciple, but the disciple should certainly also fit the guru. Whether there is such a mutual fit can rarely be decided right away except in special cases where the disciple was a student of the guru in a previous life, or initiated into a similar lineage or some similar circumstance, and there is an immediate and usually mutual recognition. Gurus can take students contrary to this of course, and usually do. Some real gurus are very picky and they do not initiate people off the street, but demand years of preparation through meditation and so on. This was usually the case with shaktipāt initiation. Now things are changing and Mother wants shaktipāt to be readily available for everybody.

THE STUDENT

The personality of the student

The true guru is generally not interested in the student's personality. He is only so as far as it hinders the student's ability to surrender to Mother Divine, or in other words, practice love, devotion and surrender to Shakti. In those cases, the guru may point out character flaws in the student, but the guru also knows that in most such cases the student will be too arrogant or narcissistic to listen anyway. In those cases, the guru mostly just keeps quiet. Many who insist on working with the personality as part of their spiritual life are so thoroughly identified with their egos, that they would not be able to embrace Shaktipāt Siddha Yoga anyway. Why work on the personality in the name of enlightenment if you have realized it is not you? Personalities do need working on of course, it is just not a way to, or prerequisite for, enlightenment. Thus, it is not part of Shaktipāt Siddha Yoga per se, though the guru usually does prick to his student's egos now and then. And the closer the bond between the student and the guru, the tougher the guru might be. This does not mean the given student has more issues than others, usually they have less. The guru just knows that if he pricks to the egos of those who are merely hanging around, they will run away screaming. Better let them hang around and hope the Shakti will grab them. Self-examination is important on this path and at the end of this book you can find a list psychological defense mechanisms that one should look out for.

Qualities and counter-qualities of a student

Ideally, the student should have a strong longing for liberation, for enlightenment, to know the true Self (as distinct from the small self). The latter is not enough in itself, because there are so many misconceptions about what the True Self is. Freud had his ideas, Jung had his, Prabhupāda had his, Shankara's writings express one, Ramanuja's another, and so on. In general, they are all wrong because all they have given or left us is nothing but text. Text can never capture the ultimate truth about the Self. Advaita (so-called *non-duality*), as far as most people understand it, is for amateurs; these followers of 'non-duality' are not even spiritual, they are just ego-tripping or engaging in mental self-gratification with an infatuated sense of being deeply spiritual – though it has no base in reality and leads nowhere. Some so called 'Tantric' students even worship the sexual orgasm as a form of samādhi (it isn't). Some even practice a form of meditation where the shakti triggers a prolonged orgasm and they think this is samādhi and deeply spiritual. They are totally deluded and such practices are to be condemned. They are merely fixating the shakti in the swādhistāna chakra (2nd chakra) and doing a masturbative kind of meditation with it there. Women are especially attracted to this; men find it more difficult since they ejaculate and it ends there. These poor souls are not only never going to make it, they are digging a pit for themselves messing up the proper working of kundalinī shakti.

The student should be willing to follow the guru's teaching and personal advice, no matter what. A student who receives shaktipāt and does not follow the guru's teaching, but either stays with, or runs off to, some other spiritual teacher, sect or movement wastes not only the shaktipāt initiation, but also a great chance for intimate, loving guidance to help him reach enlightenment. I have in my teaching experience initiated numerous who were ardent followers of some other path or guru (without me knowing they were so). It turns out they only came for shaktipāt in order to get their established sādhana to work for them; especially followers of the so called 'Kundalinī Yoga' path of the Sikhs, as promoted by the late Yogi Bhajan. So, I ask them: "Why don't you give it up, since it is not giving the desired results of samādhi?" They usually have no answer and leave me, or they try to convince me that their sādhana is the world's best sādhana. So they explain their practices and I find them ridiculous and they leave. Well, if their practices are so fantastic, why did they come to me in the first place? I have lost patience with these poor individuals, who are mostly proud of their white turbans, orange robes or grandiose spiritual names.

An ideal student is at least humble enough to question his own ideas about truth. At best, he is surrendering to growing devotion to God within. You have to understand that a true Siddha guru does not particularly want anyone to be devoted to him as a body or personality. The true guru only wants to awaken the inner guru within you and see you surrender to Him/Her. The inner guru on our path is to be thought of as Mother Divine and/or Krishna, since those are the paramgurus (originators) of our budding lineage, but in reality, the inner guru is your own unmanifest Self guiding you via kundalinī and her working in you. Mother Divine may appear to you as Virgin Mary, for example.

If all a guru can do for you is make you think, however interesting the new mental grooves may be, he is not a real guru. I am not saying a real guru will not make you think. He most certainly will challenge your mind and your ideas, but he will be able to do much more and will do so in time if you stay with him and do what he says. It is these last four words that students find the most difficult: *Do what he says.*

Deluded seekers

Most people who call themselves seekers, though they will readily admit that they are not enlightened, think they know the best way to get enlightened, at least for themselves. They are the most deluded of all students and they won't make it; they are just mentally self-gratifying or ego-tripping. Then there is the spiritual narcissist who believes gurus are there to serve him and that spirituality is a tool to make him feel great about himself and love himself more. A variation of the spiritual narcissist is the person who is more or less consciously proud of his path and thinks he has the best path in the world and that he is somehow elect since he is following that path. It is this sense of being elect, plus the self-centered nature of the spiritual search, that makes him a narcissist. Furthermore, there are two types of deluded seekers: those who have it all in the head and those who have it all in the heart. This gives us four kinds of deluded seekers:

1. The mentally self-gratifying spiritual know-it-all

2. The mentally self-gratifying spiritual narcissist

3. The loving spiritual know-it-all

4. The loving spiritual narcissist

The mentally self-gratifying spiritual know-it-all is usually a non-dualist, often quite intelligent. He is expert at refuting everything you say. He knows best and will argue along these lines: *What can be higher than the unmanifest? Emotions are in the relative, bliss is an emotion, so your blissful enlightenment is inferior to mine!* (so they argue). Interestingly, they have it all in their head and have not at all realized the unmanifest. I watched a non-dualist describe enlightenment: He explained that to him there was no longer any difference between a cheeseburger and a glass of wine. Such nonsense! Even in the unitary state you are even more so aware of the difference of forms and appearances.

The mentally self-gratifying spiritual narcissist is usually a Buddhist, an Osho follower or a 'Kundalinī Yoga' Sikh, or a follower of some other sect or religion which claims to offer true spirituality, but rarely offers much more than mental or practical stuff to boost the student's ego in the name of transcending the ego. These deluded individuals think that if they do something over and over again, they will magically become worthy of enlightenment upon which it will be given to them. Given by whom? This 'You get it when you have earned it' attitude is ruining the spiritual life of most seekers, especially in this category because they are often genuine seekers.

The loving spiritual know it all is usually an alternative therapist or a new-age inspired psychotherapist, or someone who is a workshop jumper (or, often, a mixture). They are usually not particularly intelligent, though some are. I am not saying they are dimwitted, but they rarely go much above average. They may have a good university degree but their lack of creative thinking denotes lack of genius and a truly high IQ.

The loving spiritual narcissist will look you deeply in the eyes and place his or her hand on your heart chakra and think that with all their good intentions and good motions (which they will deny is show-off, though it is), they are evolving spiritually. Of course, it is all a show put on for them to feel good about themselves and show, for all to see, how good they are. Thus, they are narcissists. They tend to live off unemployment support and justify their narcissistic idea that they are some sort of super-person that everybody else should take care of, by deluding themselves that they have a special 'resting-incarnation' or a 'mission' to help make the world more spiritual and that they could not fulfill their mission if they had to earn a living.

Ignorance is upholding a belief that you are what you are not

Here are some examples of what you are not:

You are not your body. You temporarily have a body.
You are not your thoughts or feelings.
You are not joy or misery.
You are not your personality.
You are not your ego.
You are not that which undergoes therapy.
You are not that which is worked upon in workshops.
You are not your orgasms.
You are not male, female or androgen.
You are not a clairvoyant person.
You are not a smart or dumb person.
You are not a spiritual person.
You are not a good or bad meditator.

SĀDHANA

LOVE, DEVOTION, SURRENDER

These three qualities are very important on our path. You should develop love for God in whatever form of God that appeals the most to your heart, be it Mother Divine, Virgin Mary, Jesus, Krishna or whoever. Love, devotion and surrender come in the mentioned order. Without love, you cannot feel true devotion. Without true devotion, you cannot surrender to Mother Shakti. As you progress on this path these qualities will grow in you. Shakti is the giver of devotion, the giver of love and bliss. It is impossible not to surrender to Her once She showers those upon you and awakens them in you. The more attached you are to your ignorance, the tougher the process of merging with Mother will be. That is why practicing love, devotion and surrender is alpha and omega. To be ignorant is to be devoid of bliss. Give up your ignorance and offer it to Mother. Offer your mind to Mother. Let everything you do be an act of service to Mother, an act of devotion; this is difficult unless Shakti has grabbed you, so surrender to Mother Shakti. Surrendering is also difficult if you do not feel love and devotion to Mother. Practice meditation as prescribed, pray often for your enlightenment, and soon Shakti will grab you. Pray to Mother that She will show you Her love for you. Eventually every breath you take will be an act of supreme devotion to Mother; every moment will be filled with bliss, love and devotion. Many tears will have been shed before this. Give up all desires except the desire to be filled with Mother's grace. In meditation, Mother comes to you in the form of bliss. Give up the experiencer of the bliss and merge with bliss. Let there be nothing but bliss, nothing but Mother. Supreme bliss and Mother are One. This bliss is Love Supreme.

Mother's Love for You

It is impossible to describe the sweetness of Mother's love for you.

It is impossible to describe the fierceness with which She works in you for your enlightenment.

Once you surrender to Mother, She will take care of your spiritual life, both without and within.

Sometimes like a raging fire, sometimes like a gentle caress, her love for you takes many forms.

If you ignore Her, She will quietly wait in the shadows for you to invite Her back in. She will never abandon you.

If you love Her, She will love you back tenfold.

Every tear shed out of love for Mother is, to Mother, like an ocean of devotion to Her. She swims in it.

Worldly life is a mire of disappointments. Mother will never disappoint you.

The physical body will wither and die. Mother is eternal life, bliss and freedom. Surrender to Mother!

Mother permeates everything. Find Her in everything. Everything is bliss.

Mother's bliss will devour your ignorance.

Prayer to Mother

I am on fire with Mother.
I have drowned in Mother's tears.
Fire and tears – at once?
Her tears of love for me
are boiling liquids of bliss.
Her raging fire in me
is aching acidic fluids of devotion.
Oh my! Who can I pray to for help
when there is nothing beyond You?
Who can I serve to make me worthy
of what is my very Self?
Oh Mother! Kill me! Kill me! Kill me!

Excerpts from Narada's Bhakti Sutras

2. Bhakti has the form of intense love towards God.

3. nd the form of Amrita [the bliss of the absolute Self].

4. By attaining which a man becomes a Siddha and completely satisfied.

16. According to Sandilya devotion may be indicated by unhindered enjoyment of bliss, caused by the love of God.

26. The result of devotion is more devotion.

30. Devotion is its own fruit.

36. Devotion is most effectively cultivated by unceasing adoration and remembrance of God.

38. But devotion is acquired chiefly and surely by the grace of the Great Ones or the touch of Divine compassion.

51. The real nature of love of God cannot be described but is a matter of experience.

53. The real, intense devotion appears by itself in a devotee who is ready.

54. This real devotion is beyond the gunas, is devoid of personal desire, it increases steadily by itself and exists in the subtlest realms of Being. It has to be experienced to be known.

55. Having attained this highest state of devotion, the devotee sees nothing but God, hears nothing but God and thinks of nothing but God.

60. One result of this devotion is utter peace of mind and a mind filled with supreme bliss.

70. Having merged into oneness with the Absolute.

80. Being earnestly invoked through supreme devotion, God reveals Himself without delay and fills the devotee with Himself.

Three classes of devotees

There are three kinds of bhaktas (devotees of God), in descending order:

1. **Sattvic devotees**. Those who are so full of love for God that they do not care how they live. Their home may be a mess; they see it all as God. They do not care about their clothes or their social status. They are satisfied with having enough income to support them and nothing more. All they do is love God throughout the day and the night. Their hearts overflow constantly and they feel God walks with them all the time. Their altar may be a dusty mess and their meditation room untidy. They meditate everywhere with the same surrender.

2. **Rajasic devotees**. Those who worship god and ask for boons and blessings. They pray fervently to god. Their home is nice and tidy and their altar and meditation room is always clean and shiny. They pray to god during the appointed hours and perform rituals, ceremonies and vows. They believe they have to earn god's favors, so they do what they can to earn them. They beg and cry and fall on the floor. They make a show of how much they love the Lord and think the more devotional acts they perform the more they will deserve God's love.

3. **Tamasic devotees**. These perform the devotional acts for the sake of public appearance. They use devotion as a means to advance in social status. They know it is good to be a devotee, so they act like devotees in order to score points in society. They may be good at singing kirtans, but their driving motive is pride. Those of rajasic devotion may follow them, but those of sattvic devotion shun them as evil fakes even though they may sing well, have nice voices and so on.

Spiritual Practices

The most important spiritual practice for a Shaktipāt Siddha yoga initiate is simply to surrender to the shakti and merge in bliss.

If you are not there yet, you could do some of the spiritual practices described in the following to purify the system and invite kundalinī shakti to rise and shower you with the blissful grace of the Divine Mother.

How to Meditate

Before we go into the various techniques, take note of this: No technique will ever take you to liberation. If you want to reach nirvikalpa samādhi, which is samadhi devoid (*nir*) of fluctuations (*vikalpas*) of the mind and consciousness, you have to understand that any meditation practice or spiritual practice is in itself a *vikalpa*, a fluctuation. You have to let go of the technique and merge with the Self at the right time. I usually tell my students that the meditation technique is like a train ride; it takes you to the destination, but you have to get off the train at the destination to remain there, otherwise the train (technique) will remove you from your destination again. I normally suggest doing Kundalinī Kriyā and/or Kriyā Prānāyāma as the main practice, to be done twice daily for 20-50 minutes. If you don't have the time for that, do as much as you can manage. If Kundalinī Kriyā generates too much pressure in the head, stop doing it and do Kriyā Prānāyāma instead. Or try the remedy below. Pressure in the various chakras is nothing to be alarmed about, it is a symptom of the shakti working on blockages and releasing contractions. Practicing love, devotion and surrender always helps.

Beginning and ending meditation

Warm-up, 3 - 5 minutes
Sit comfortably in an upright posture. Go through your body beginning with the feet and ending with the head. Feel your feet, but in such a manner that you don't do it from your head down, but

rather are present in the feet and let the feet feel themselves. Let your whole attention be filled with the sensation of the feet. Then proceed to the ankles, the calves, and so forth. Spend as much time in each place as is needed in order to feel the presence there. When you reach the head, then feel the entire body. Do the Light Body technique. Notice the body is breathing by itself. Don't interfere with the rhythm, simply observe it.

Ending meditation

When it's time to end meditation, don't just stop and get up. First, let go, and see if you don't go deeper by letting go. Spend some time like this. Do Aura Luminance. Then, when you really want to stop, sit with closed eyes a while and slowly open them while staying in meditation. Or, if you don't want to open them slowly, you can open and close your eyes a few times while trying to hold the meditative state. Then meditate a few minutes with open eyes. Notice how your state is different now from what it was just before you began meditating. Remember, we don't go out of meditation since meditation is merging with the Self, and we don't want to go out of the Self. Rather we take meditation into the waking state.

THE MEDITATION TECHNIQUES

The Light Body

Do this for a few minutes before you meditate and when you end meditation. Keep it in the back of your mind while you meditate without letting it disturb your meditation, of course.

Imagine your body is a source of light, like a strong light-bulb. Sense the entire body all the way down to the feet is radiant white light. Imagine the while light spread around your body in a large oval shaped space. It fills the space around your body with blazing white light. If it comes natural to you to use bright cyan or luminous gold, that is fine..

Kundalinī Kriyā

The practice consists of three methods, which you switch between. When you reach a plateau, you switch to one of the other methods, and when that reaches a plateau, you switch back to the first method or to the next method, and so forth. Back and forth between the three main techniques, but all the while having just one objective: To intensify Shakti more and more and to merge with it.

1. Body breathing
As you observe the breathing, feel the entire body. It is as if the sense of touch built into the skin senses the skin itself. Now feel on the in-breath that you expand out through the skin. On the out-breath simply let go. Another way of saying it, is that on the in-breath you feel the Shakti growing in intensity and size. On the out-breath you let go of any control or duality and merge with Shakti in and around the body. As this continues, you will feel the body's limits dissolve, while the feeling of Shakti becomes more tangible than the feeling of the body. Do this for as long as Shakti gets stronger, and you merge more and more. When it reaches a plateau, switch to spinal breathing.

2. Spinal breathing
On the in-breath, feel that you are moving energy up the entire spine at once, from the perineum to the top of the head. You can think of the Divine Mother as you do this and can remember the mantra *Om* (or *Am*) as you do this. On the out-breath, feel that you are radiating energy, or lovebliss, in all directions from the brain and scull. You can think of Mother Divine and can remember the mantra *Kreem* (or *Ma*) as you breathe out. But these words are really not the most important. The most important thing is to feel Shakti grow and to merge with Shakti. Shakti is Mother Divine (Amma). Do this as long as Shakti gets stronger and you merge more and more. When it reaches a plateau, return to full body

breathing. If you feel the energy pressure in the head becomes unpleasantly high, replace this practice with Kriyā Prānāyāma. *Kreem* is the seed mantra for Mother Kali, the destroyer of ignorance.

3. Merging inflow and outflow
Here you do not follow the breath, but sense Shakti flows *into* the entire body and radiates *from* the entire body at the same time. This can be a rather paradoxical feeling, but once you get the knack of it, it is a very powerful meditation. Another way to explain it is to say you should sense radiating love to everything around you and receiving love from everything around you at the same time.

Merging in Lovebliss
When you experience being filled with Shakti or Lovebliss, then let go of your methods and merge with it. This is the goal of all practices and methods. No matter what practice you are doing, if you are on the verge of transcending I-ness and merging, then let go of the method/practice and merge in Lovebliss.

Remedy for pressure in the head

If too much energy builds up in the head during meditation, you can try this: During the second practice of Kundalinī Kriyā, on the in-breath you could bring the shakti up to the crown via the spine, then hold the breath a short while and bring the shakti from the head down the Amrita nādi to the heart (this nādi goes from the top of the head down the front of the face and throat to the middle of the chest), then on the out-breath expand the heart chakra. While holding the breath, it is important to let go of all contractions in the brain. Alternatively, stop doing Kundalinī Kriyā and do Kriyā Prānāyāma instead. Or just do *body breathing* and *merging in lovebliss* and skip *spinal breathing* for a while. Or meditate on love, devotion, surrender in the heart chakra as explained below. Or skip the technique that generates pressure in the head and do any of the below prānāyāmas instead, in particular *5-5 Pranayama*. under *Additional Practices*. Or replace spinal breathing with Kriyā Prānāyāma so you move up and down.

Kriyā Prāṇāyāma (Spinal Breathing, Vertical Breathing)

Calmly follow your breath. Do not try to manipulate it to be longer than what it spontaneously is. Do not do ujjayi prāṇāyāma unless it comes natural or you are sure it really improves the practice. Focus on the Sushumnā nādi that goes from the perineum to the top of the head through the center of the spine.

On the in-breath sense energy rising up inside Sushumnā to the top of the scull. If you do not make it all the way, don't bother or think you are doing something wrong. But try to move energy a little faster sometime in the future when it feels comfortable, so you can get it all the way up.

On the out-breath sense energy descending down to the perineum again.

There is a somewhat peculiar mantra one should use:

On the **in-breath** mentally think, or merely remember the mantra *hong* (pronounced [hɔŋ:]). You can also pronounce it *hung* [huŋ:]. I find both work well. *Hong/Hung* has the power to awaken kundalini.

On the **out-breath** mentally think the mantra *sauḥ* [sɔ:] (pronounced like the English word 'saw'). *Sauh* has the power of activating the kundalini awakened by *hong*.

This is the secret hamsa practice that Lord Bhairava (Shiva) hints at at the very end of the Vijñānabhairava Tantra. The mantra *hong* (or *hung*) is an ancient Tantric *bija-mantra* that stimulates kundalinī to awaken. Some maintain the mantra should be 'ham' and 'sa', but they are misguided. Hamsa is the name of the mantra; its pronunciation has usually been kept secret.

Kundalinī Prāṇāyāma (3-3-3 Prāṇāyāma)

A prāṇāyāma is a breathing exercise. The focus of the practice is not so much the control of prāna (vital-force), but the awakening and arousal of kundalinī. The purpose of this is to generate Shakti-bliss on which you can surf into the Self and merge awareness and Shakti into Pure Being.

Sit in a comfortable position and do the preparations for meditation as described above.

There is a special breathing-cycle to this, which it is important to keep. It has three steps: Breathing in, holding the breath and breathing out. It is very important that all three phases are of equal duration. It is also important to keep the rhythm going steadily at the same pace, so you should find a duration that suits you well and is comfortable and relaxed.

You could count to three repeatedly in the same rhythm (or whatever number is appropriate). It is important not to get tense, so one should find a comfortable number and rhythm you can keep steadily for 10 to 50 minutes without getting out of breath or feeling you are enforcing control over the breath. Enforcing control will not do any good at all, and in fact, it will block the intended result. It should be a nice, calm, peaceful cycle.

1. **On the in-breath** imagine and feel shakti moving from the perineum up inside the entire spine to the top of the head. Do not imagine it as a point going up, but more like a flow in the entire channel. You can mentally think the mantra *Om*.

2. **Hold your breath** in a comfortable and relaxed manner. Meanwhile, imagine/feel the energy in the brain radiate in all directions. You can mentally think the mantra *Aim*.

3. **On the out-breath** continue radiating shakti in all directions from the brain. You can mentally think the mantra *Kreem*.

That is one round. Find a speed of counting and number (or use the mantras in equal duration) that ensures you can, in a relaxed manner, do a lot of rounds without interruption.

Alternatives:
1. On the out-breath, simply let go of any effort that may have been involved and merge with the shakti present in and around the body. You can use the same mantra (Kreem).

2. Or, on the out-breath, sense/imagine energy flowing down inside the spine and striking kundalinī in the perineum, waking Her up so she will rise on the next in-breath. Mentally think the mantra hung inside the root chakra.

Soon you will find that shakti moves up the spine and radiates out from the brain at the same time and does so on the in-breath, while holding the breath and on the out-breath. That is a good sign and you should keep with that.

Beware that this practice is for awakening and arousing kundalini. You may experience this as something moving in your spine, or heat in the spine, but do not be alarmed. If you find it releases more energy than you are comfortable with, then also do not be alarmed, for it will soon calm down and integrate with the system.

Also, note that you may not feel anything up the spine but will feel a lot when radiating from the brain. Know that even though you felt nothing up the spine, if you feel it radiating from the brain it flowed up inside the spine as it should.

ADDITIONAL PRACTICES

Chakra Kriyā

This can be done in any chakra, but is usually done in the heart chakra (middle of the chest), or in the ājnā chakra (between the eyebrows). If you want to do a nice and very powerful systematic method, you can go through all the chakras in order, beginning at the bottom and moving up one at a time. It has four steps to be performed in each chakra.

1. Pulsating
On the in-breath, sense energy going forward from the spine to the front of the body, and on the out-breath, moving back into the spine. Do this for about ten breaths. (If working with the root chakra or crown chakra, sense the energy moving up on the in-breath and down on the out-breath.)

2. Expanding
Sense the entire chakra as a tube from the spine to the front of the body, or as a ball large enough to reach both the front and back. Or sense a ball the size of a fist in the front of the body. On the in-breath sense it expanding, and on the out-breath simply let go. Do this for about ten breaths.

3. Radiating
Sense energy, love and bliss radiate from the chakra in all directions. Do this for about ten breaths.

4. Changing chakra
If you want to do a systematic practice for awakening the entire chakra system, then this is how to shift from one chakra to the next. On the in-breath, feel energy rising up the spine from the chakra you are leaving and reaching the next chakra. On the out-breath, feel the new chakra expanding. Do these for about ten breaths, and then proceed to the next chakra.

As you do this practice you may feel pressure in the body, in the chakra areas. Also, hidden emotions may arise. Please allow whatever comes up to arise, to be what it is, and leave. Remember that the goal is not catharsis, but to generate a pulse of shakti on which you can surf into bliss and the Self.

Chakra Mantra Meditation

This is a potent practice. Go through all the chakras one at a time. Mentally repeat the relevant mantra once in each chakra in turn. Begin with Ājnā chakra between the eyebrows, then work your way down the front of the body, chakra by chakra, to Mulādhāra in the perineum. Then work your way up the spine, chakra by chakra, placing the Ājnā at the back of the head and Sahasrāra on the top of the head. This is one round, do at least three rounds. Feel love and devotion to Mother when you mentally repeat the mantras in each chakra. "Shri Matre Namaha" expresses that devotion. Use the following mantras:

Chakra	Mantra
7. Sahasrāra	Aum Sauh Hoom Shri Matre Namaha Aum
6. Ājnā	Om Haum Hleem Shri Matre Namaha Om
5. Vishuddhi	Ham Om Kreem Shri Matre Namaha Ham
4. Anāhata	Yam Om Gaum Shri Matre Namaha Yam
3. Manipura	Ram Om Aim Shri Matre Namaha Ram
2. Swādhistāna	Vam Om Hreem Shri Matre Namaha Vam
1. Mulādhāra	Lam Om Shreem Shri Matre Namaha Lam

Simple Prānāyāma (Pranayama nr. 2)

This is the simplest prānāyāma. If you are feeling drowsy during meditation, or during the day, doing it a few minutes can often help clear the mind. You alternately breathe in through one nostril and out through the other. Use the thumb and another finger to block the nostril you are not breathing in or out of. One round has six steps:

1. Breathe in through the left nostril. You think the mantra *Shreem*.

2. Hold the breath a short moment as you change nostril.

3. Breathe out through the right nostril. You can think the mantra *Hreem*.

4. Breathe in through the right nostril. You can think the mantra *Hreem*.

5. Hold the breath a short moment as you change nostril.

6. Breathe out through the left nostril. You can think the mantra *Shreem*.

That is one round. Do as many rounds as you feel like.

Prānāyāma Nr. 5

Like the Simple Pranayama, this is good to do when feeling drowsy during meditation. Breathe in through both nostrils, then block the left nostril with a finger (press on the side of the nose) and breathe out through the right nostril. Do this for five breaths (always breathing out through the right nostril). Then continue breathing in through both nostrils, but now breathe out through the left nostril by blocking the right nostril with a finger (by pressing on the side of the nose). Do this for five breaths (always breathing out through the left nostril). This is one round. Do as many rounds as you are comfortable with.

PRĀNĀYĀMAS

Nr. 1. Kriyā Prānāyāma

Spinal Breathing, Vertical Breathing

Calmly follow your breath. Do not try to manipulate it to be longer than what it spontaneously is. Do not do ujjayi prānāyāma unless it comes natural or you are sure it really improves the practice. Focus on the Sushumnā nādi that goes from the perineum to the top of the head through the center of the spine.

On the in-breath sense energy rising up inside Sushumnā to the top of the scull. If you do not make it all the way, don't bother or think you are doing something wrong. But try to move energy a little faster sometime in the future when it feels comfortable, so you can get it all the way up.

On the out-breath sense energy descending down to the perineum again.

There is a somewhat peculiar mantra one should use:

On the **in-breath** mentally think, or merely remember the mantra *hong* (pronounced [hɔŋ:]). You can also pronounce it *hung* [huŋ:]. I find both work well. *Hong/Hung* has the power to awaken kundalini.

On the **out-breath** mentally think the mantra *sauḥ* [sɔ:] (pronounced like the English word 'saw'). *Sauḥ* has the power of activating the kundalini awakened by *hong*.

This is the secret hamsa practice that Lord Bhairava (Shiva) hints at at the very end of the Vijñānabhairava Tantra. The mantra *hong* (or *hung*) is an ancient Tantric *bija-mantra* that stimulates kundalinī to awaken. Some maintain the mantra should be 'ham' and 'sa', but they are misguided. Hamsa is the name of the mantra; its pronunciation has usually been kept secret.

Nr. 2. Simple Prānāyāma

This is the simplest prānāyāma. If you are feeling drowsy during meditation, or during the day, doing it a few minutes can often help clear the mind. You alternately breathe in through one nostril and out through the other. Use the thumb and another finger to block the nostril you are not breathing in or out of. One round has six steps:

1. Breathe in through the left nostril. You think the mantra *Shreem*.

2. Hold the breath a short moment as you change nostril.

3. Breathe out through the right nostril. You can think the mantra *Hreem*.

4. Breathe in through the right nostril. You can think the mantra *Hreem*.

5. Hold the breath a short moment as you change nostril.

6. Breathe out through the left nostril. You can think the mantra *Shreem*.

That is one round. Do as many rounds as you feel like.

Nr. 3. Kundalinī Prānāyāma (3-3-3 Prānāyāma)

A prānāyāma is a breathing exercise. The focus of the practice is not so much the control of prāna (vital-force), but the awakening and arousal of kundalinī. The purpose of this is to generate Shakti-bliss on which you can surf into the Self and merge awareness and Shakti into Pure Being.

Sit in a comfortable position and do the preparations for meditation as described above.

There is a special breathing-cycle to this, which it is important to keep. It has three steps: Breathing in, holding the breath and breathing out. It is very important that all three phases are of equal duration. It is also important to keep the rhythm going steadily at the same pace, so you should find a duration that suits you well and is comfortable and relaxed.

You could count to three repeatedly in the same rhythm (or whatever number is appropriate). It is important not to get tense, so one should find a comfortable number and rhythm you can keep steadily for 10 to 50 minutes without getting out of breath or feeling you are enforcing control over the breath. Enforcing control will not do any good at all, and in fact, it will block the intended result. It should be a nice, calm, peaceful cycle.

1. **On the in-breath** imagine and feel shakti moving from the perineum up inside the entire spine to the top of the head. Do not imagine it as a point going up, but more like a flow in the entire channel. You can mentally think the mantra *Om*.

2. **Hold your breath** in a comfortable and relaxed manner. Meanwhile, imagine/feel the energy in the brain radiate in all directions. You can mentally think the mantra *Aim*.

3. **On the out-breath** continue radiating shakti in all directions from the brain. You can mentally think the mantra *Kreem*.

That is one round. Find a speed of counting and number (or use the mantras in equal duration) that ensures you can, in a relaxed manner, do a lot of rounds without interruption.

Alternatives:

1. On the out-breath, simply let go of any effort that may have been involved and merge with the shakti present in and around the body. You can use the same mantra (*Kreem*).

2. Or, on the out-breath, sense/imagine energy flowing down inside the spine and striking kundalinī in the perineum, waking Her up so she will rise on the next in-breath. Mentally think the mantra *hung* inside the root chakra.

Soon you will find that shakti moves up the spine and radiates out from the brain at the same time and does so on the in-breath, while holding the breath and on the out-breath. That is a good sign and you should keep with that.

Beware that this practice is for awakening and arousing kundalinī. You may experience this as something moving in your spine, or heat in the spine, but do not be alarmed. If you find it releases more energy than you are comfortable with, then also do not be alarmed, for it will soon calm down and integrate with the system.

Also, note that you may not feel anything up the spine but will feel a lot when radiating from the brain. Know that even though you felt nothing up the spine, if you feel it radiating from the brain it flowed up inside the spine as it should.

Nr. 4. Bhastrika (bellows)

Simple Bhastrika Prānāyāma

Warning: Do not do this if you are pregnant!

1. Sit comfortably, with the spine fairly erect. Cross-legged on the floor or in lotus posture or half lotus is ideal.

2. Close the mouth and breathe through the nostrils a few times in a relaxed manner.

3. When you are relaxed and ready, forcibly and quickly breathe in and out of the nostrils by expanding the chest and belly and contracting them again. Do this 10-20 times (whatever you are comfortable with, start with a low number).

4. Then take a deep breath and hold the breath as long as you comfortably can while still being able to exhale relaxed.

5. Exhale relaxed. Then take a deep breath and relax a few moments.

Advanced Bhastrika Prānāyāma

Warning: Do not do this if you are pregnant!

This extremely potent prānāyāma is usually kept secret. It is only recommended for initiates into Shaktipāt Siddha Yoga, and only for those who either already have their kundalinī awakened, or who don't have an awakened kundalinī and wish to awaken kundalinī.

1. Preferably sit cross-legged on the floor. The lotus posture or half lotus is best. If you cannot do this, sit on a firm chair, without reclining against its back, and spread your knees.

2. Place the palms of hands on the knees, fingers facing forward, not outward. Bend your arms slightly and lean slightly forward so the weight of the torso is distributed between the spine and the hands. The head will sink down between the shoulders as if slumping a bit forward and the shoulders rising.

3. Take a deep, relaxed breath and exhale in a relaxed manner. Close the mouth.

4. Breathe rapidly and fairly deeply through the nose (as described under bhastrika above) for a number of breaths (7-10 is good for beginners; with practice, you can increase to 20-30).

5. Take a deep in-breath.

6. Do moola bandha.

7. Do a modified version of uddīyāna bandha: With full lungs hold your breath; contract the abdomen and pull it in with a 'vacuum in-breath'. Sense shakti rising up inside the spine. You can also do it with empty lungs; whatever works best.

8. Do jālandhara bandha and keep sensing kundalinī shakti rising up inside the spine and filling the brain. Feel it radiating from the brain in all directions.

9. Hold 6, 7 and 8 as long as it is comfortable, while radiating shakti, bliss, light, love and devotion, from the brain in all directions. Do not hold the breath so long that you feel you are suffocating or have to quickly exhale and inhale to catch your breath.

10. Gently release and exhale. Take a deep breath and relax.

11. Sit with closed eyes and radiate shakti, bliss, light, devotion, etc., from the brain or the whole body in all directions for a few minutes. Breathe in a natural, relaxed manner. Remain erect, but relax the body. Merge into bliss.

This is one round. Do 2-5 rounds. Beginners should only do one or two.

Nr. 5. (5-5 Prānāyāma)

Like the Simple Prānāyāma, this is good to do when feeling drowsy during meditation. Breathe in through both nostrils, then block the left nostril with a finger (press on the side of the nose) and breathe out through the right nostril. Do this for five breaths (right nostril for all five out-breaths). Then continue breathing in through both nostrils, but now breathe out through the left nostril by blocking the right nostril with a finger (by pressing on the side of the nose). Do this for five breaths (left nostril for all five out-breaths). This is one round. Do as many rounds as you are comfortable with.

MANTRA YOGA ADDENDA

In our tradition, we are mainly concerned with Shakti mantras, and mainly their bija (seed) form. In particular, there are eleven mantras that we can use: *Aum, Om, Aim, Hreem, Shreem, Kreem, Kleem, Huum, Hleem, Streem* and *Treem*. They all invoke various aspects of Shakti, our beloved Divine Mother. You can use any of them alone or in combinations. The most important ones are *Om*, *Aim* and *Hreem*. They are often used together in that order, after which you can add mantras for the deities or qualities you wish to invoke, like in *Om Aim Hreem Sreem Om*. Or you can use the individual mantra alone or in combination with *Om*.

Aum

Aum [aum:] is specifically associated with the Sahasrāra chakra. See *Om*.

Om

Om [oum:] is a universal mantra that invokes the Purusha (the Absolute), Ishvara (the Divine Being), the Primal spirit, Pure Consciousness – depending on your personal tendency and how you understand the highest. Amongst the Hindu deities, Om refers to Shiva, the perfect yogi eternally in samādhi. Most combined mantras begin with *Om*. When working with the lower chakras we normally use *Om* in combinations, but we use *Aum* with the Sahasrāra chakra. Apart from that the meaning of *Om* and *Aum* is the same. *Om* is associated with the Ājnā chakra.

Aim

Aim [aim:] is the mantra of Adya Shakti (Primal Shakti or cosmic feminine force as Mother Divine). *Om* and *Aim* are considered counterparts, like Shiva and Shakti, and often go together in mantras. This mantra is second in importance to *Om* and many mantras begin with *Om aim*. Specifically, *Aim* is the bija mantra of Sarasvati, the manifestation of Mother as the embodiment of knowledge, learning and speech. She is the granter of wisdom and higher understanding. *Aim* is also the mantra of the guru-principle and invokes the inner guru. It is associated with Manipura chakra.

Hreem

Hreem [hri:m:] is the prime mantra of the Divine Mother in general. It indicates Shakti's power of creation, preservation and destruction. It brings ecstasy and bliss. It purifies the heart and develops devotion in us and longing for merging with Mother Divine. Specifically, it refers to Parvati, Shiva's spouse, who is the goddess of love and devotion. *Hreem* is solar. It is associated with Swādhistāna chakra.

Shreem

Shreem [ʃriːmː] invokes Mother's benevolent sides, such as prosperity, growth and material wealth. Specifically, it refers to Lakshmi. *Shreem* also refers to Rama, the upholder of righteousness. *Shreem* also invokes faith, devotion and surrender. *Shreem* is lunar. It is associated with Mulādhāra chakra.

Kreem

Kreem [kriːmː] refers to the kriyā shakti, the force behind motion and activity. Specifically, it is the mantra of Kali, the merciless destroyer of ignorance. Kali was the perfect female yogini; hence she is very dear to yogis. She destroys ignorance and brings transformation. *Kreem* is a mantra for awakening kundalinī (along with Hong/Hung). *Kreem* can have very harsh effects as it is quite merciless in destroying ignorance, especially if it is used in combination with *Hreem*. It is associated with Vishuddhi chakra.

Kleem

Kleem [kliːmː] is a softer version of *Kreem*. Specifically, the mantra relates to both Krishna and Sundari, the goddess of love and attraction. Krishna is the avatar of love who draws his devotees into bliss. So *Kleem* evokes love and devotion and draws the yogi into those qualities within.

Huum, Hum (Hung/Hong)

Huum [huːmː] and *Hum* [humː]. Specifically, like *Kreem*, they refer to Kali, the goddess who destroys ignorance and grants enlightenment, they are gentler than *Kreem*, though. They are used for raising kundalinī, in which case it can be pronounced *hung* or *hong*.

Hleem

Hleem [hliːmː] is a mantra of bliss, of ānanda. It is mainly a mantra to stop negative energies or things in motion. It can be used to stop negative thoughts or mind patterns. It is used to give control over the mind, to stop thoughts.

Streem

Streem [stri:m:] is a shanti mantra. Specifically it refers to the form of Mother known as Tara or Durga,. She is protective, and also represents worldly power.

Treem

Treem [tri:m:] is another version of the Tara mantra *Streem*. It is used to overcome obstacles, but otherwise it is similar to *Streem*. It embodies the power to transcend.

Sauh, Saum

Sauh [sɔ:h] as in the mantra *hong-sauh* we use in Kriyā Prānayāma. In Kashmir Shaivism, s*auh* is considered the highest mantra along with *Om*. It refers to the highest reality as Mother. It has the power to set Shakti in motion which is why it is used in Kriyā Prānayāma along with *hong* that awakens kundalinī.

Mantras often have *Om* added like in the mantra *Om Hreem Om*, which is a basic mantra for invoking Mother. Or they are used in combination, like in the heart mantra *Yam Om Gaum Shri Matre Namaha Yam*, which is a potent heart chakra mantra. *Shri Matre Namaha* is an invocation of and devotion to the Divine Mother.

How to Use Mantras

Transcendental Meditation Style. Mentally repeat, or gently remember, the mantra. Single mantras, such as *Hreem*, usually work the best, or in combination with Om as in *Om Hreem Om*. The so called 'advanced' Transcendental Meditation mantras would be *Shri Hreem Namaha*. As the mantra repetition becomes more and more subtle you may eventually reach close to the Absolute and be in a state ecstasy or bliss. At that point let go of the mantra and merge into the Self.

In the chakras. You can work on individual chakras with the respective mantra (see table below). Mentally repeat the relevant mantra in the chakra on the front of the body. Or if it works best in the spine, you can do that. Or go back and forth between the front and the back , repeat the mantra 5-7 times at the front and 5-7 times at the back.

Chakra Mantra Meditation

This is a very potent practice. Go through all the chakras one at a time. Mentally repeat the relevant mantra once in each chakra in turn. Begin with Ājnā chakra between the eyebrows, then work your way down the front of the body, chakra by chakra, to Mulādhāra in the perineum. Then work your way up the spine, chakra by chakra, placing the Ājnā at the back of the head and Sahasrāra on the top of the head. This is one round, do at least three rounds. Feel love and devotion to Mother when you mentally repeat the mantras in each chakra. "Shri Matre Namaha" expresses that devotion. Use the following mantras:

Chakra	Mantra
7. Sahasrāra	Aum Sauh Hoom Shri Matre Namaha Aum
6. Ājnā	Om Haum Hleem Shri Matre Namaha Om
5. Vishuddhi	Ham Om Kreem Shri Matre Namaha Ham
4. Anāhata	Yam Om Gaum Shri Matre Namaha Yam
3. Manipura	Ram Om Aim Shri Matre Namaha Ram
2. Swādhistāna	Vam Om Hreem Shri Matre Namaha Vam
1. Mulādhāra	Lam Om Shreem Shri Matre Namaha Lam

KUNDALINĪ YOGA ADDENDA

Any of these practices can happen spontaneously during meditation; which is fine and should not be pushed away. One can do them voluntarily now and then. But one should not make too much of a regular practice out of them, since that will interfere with the free activities of Mother Shakti and her workings in you for your liberation.

Khechari Mudrā

This is a good habit to get into, but if you begin your meditation with it and it drops off, no problem. Sometimes not doing it and breathing through the mouth is appropriate, sometimes khechari mudrā is appropriate. But remember, the activities of Shakti and surrendering to Her is all-important.

Full Khechari mudrā:
Here the tongue is long enough to fold back and get placed above the velum so it enters into the nasal cavity at the back of the mouth (the nasopharynx). If you cannot do this, do not worry; most can't. I can't. Some sects of hatha yoga and kundalinī yoga cut the root of the tongue in order to be able to perform it. Fortunately, we do not need anything like that. The following light version works just fine:

Khechari mudrā light:
1. Moisten the lips with the tongue (if they are dry air will come in).
2. Close the mouth.
3. Simultaneously create a vacuum in the mouth by swallowing a little saliva; sucking out the air; lightly press the tip of the tongue against the back of front teeth; lightly press the top of the tongue against the palate, then swallow. The tongue should

now be stuck, due to the vacuum, to the palate, but in a relaxed manner. It can be good to begin meditation like this, then let whatever happens, happen.

Shāmbhavi Mudrā (third eye gazing)

Eyes closed. The eyes look upwards towards the third eye or the bridge of the nose. Do not strain to get the eyes as far back and centered as possible. Be gentle and relaxed.

Agochari Mudrā (nose tip gazing)

Eyes closed. The eyes focus on the tip of the nose. Be gentle and relaxed.

Moola Bandha

Warning: When overdone, you can get hemorrhoids from it! But done incidentally it can give nice results.

Contract first the genitals, then the perineum, then the anus (in that order and in rapid succession, while holding all three). When you contract anus, hold the tension and sense shakti is being sent up through Sushumnā to the top of the brain. Also, sense sexual energy is being transmuted into spiritual energy and is rushing up inside the spine.

Ujjayī Prānāyāma

Do not do this during group meditation, since the noise it creates can be disturbing to others.

1. Close your mouth and breathe in a normal, spontaneous rhythm through the nose.

2. Gently perform a slight contraction of the glottis (top of the throat) so that a slight, soft 'wheezing' sound is produced there. Do not create the sound in the nose like when snoring.

Some like to do this, incidentally, when they are doing Kriyā Prānāyāma, or during the second part of the Kundalinī Kriyā.

Jālandhara Bandha (throat lock)

This is basically very simple.

1. Preferably sit cross-legged on the floor. The lotus posture or half lotus is best. If you cannot do this, sit on a firm chair, without reclining against its back, and spread your legs.

2. Place the palms of hands on the knees, fingers facing forward, not outward. Bend your arms slightly and lean slightly forward so the weight of the torso is distributed between the spine and the hands. The head will sink down between the shoulders as if slumping a bit forward and the shoulders rising.

3. Bend the head forward so that the chin touches the top of the chest (if possible, keep it comfortable and only do it as far as you can without forcing it).

Uddīyāna Bandha (abdominal contraction)

Warning: Do not do this if you are pregnant!

1. Preferably sit cross-legged on the floor. The lotus posture or half lotus is best. If you cannot do this, sit on a firm chair, without reclining against its back, and spread your knees.

2. Place the palms of hands on the knees, fingers facing forward, not outward. Bend your arms slightly and lean slightly forward so the weight of the torso is distributed between the spine and the hands. The head will sink down between the shoulders as if slumping a bit forward and the shoulders rising.

3. Take a deep, relaxed breath and completely exhale in a relaxed manner.

4. Pull the abdomen in (and, if possible, up under the lower ribs if you are slim) by a combination of using the abdominal muscles and a slight inhalation (with the air-passages closed).

5. Hold your breath in this position as long as it is comfortable.

Bhastrika Prānāyāma (bellows breath)

Warning: Do not do this if you are pregnant!

1. Sit comfortably, with the spine fairly erect. Cross-legged on the floor or in lotus posture or half lotus is ideal.

2. Close the mouth and breathe through the nostrils a few times in a relaxed manner.

3. When you are relaxed and ready, forcibly and quickly breathe in and out of the nostrils by expanding the chest and belly and contracting them again. Do this 10-20 times (whatever you are comfortable with, start with a low number).

4. Then take a deep breath and hold the breath as long as you comfortably can while still being able to exhale relaxed.

5. Exhale relaxed. Then take a deep breath and relax a few moments.

Advanced Bhastrika Prāṇāyāma

Warning: Do not do this if you are pregnant!

This extremely potent prāṇāyāma is usually kept secret. It is only recommended for initiates into Shaktipāt Siddha Yoga, and only for those who either already have their kundalinī awakened, or who don't have an awakened kundalinī and wish to awaken kundalinī.

1. Preferably sit cross-legged on the floor. The lotus posture or half lotus is best. If you cannot do this, sit on a firm chair, without reclining against its back, and spread your knees.

2. Place the palms of hands on the knees, fingers facing forward, not outward. Bend your arms slightly and lean slightly forward so the weight of the torso is distributed between the spine and the hands. The head will sink down between the shoulders as if slumping a bit forward and the shoulders rising.

3. Take a deep, relaxed breath and exhale in a relaxed manner. Close the mouth.

4. Breathe rapidly and fairly deeply through the nose (as described under bhastrika prāṇāyāma) for a number of breaths (7-10 is good for beginners; with practice, you can increase to 20-30).

5. Take a deep in-breath.

6. Do moola bandha.

7. Do a modified version of uddīyāna bandha: With full lungs hold your breath; contract the abdomen and pull it in with a 'vacuum in-breath'. Sense shakti rising up inside the spine. You can also do it with empty lungs; whatever works best.

8. Do jālandhara bandha and keep sensing kundalinī shakti rising up inside the spine and filling the brain. Feel it radiating from the brain in all directions.

9. Hold 6, 7 and 8 as long as it is comfortable, while radiating shakti, bliss, light, love and devotion, from the brain in all directions. Do not hold the breath so long that you feel you are suffocating or have to quickly exhale and inhale to catch your breath.

10. Gently release and exhale. Take a deep breath and relax.

11. Sit with closed eyes and radiate shakti, bliss, light, devotion, etc., from the brain or the whole body in all directions for a few minutes. Breathe in a natural, relaxed manner. Remain erect, but relax the body. Merge into bliss.

This is one round. Do 2-5 rounds. Beginners should only do one or two.

HATHA YOGA ADDENDA

While we normally do not include (nor exclude) *āsanas* (yoga postures) in Shaktipāt Siddha Yoga since Mother Shakti takes care of everything, it can be nice to do the sūrya namaskar (salutation to the sun) in the morning.

Sūrya namaskar

1. Stand with your feet together. Join the palms in front of the chest. Look straight forward. Take a few relaxed breaths and get centered with the weight evenly distributed on both feet. Exhale.

2. As you inhale, raise the arms above the head. Bend backwards and push the pelvis forward. Do not bend the head backwards, but keep it between the arms. The palms no longer join, but should still face each other.

3. As you exhale, bend forward to bring your hands to the floor so the toes and fingers are in line. Try to keep the back straight so you bend at the waist. If possible, let the forehead touch the knees. If you cannot do this, you can bend the knees a little.

4. As you inhale, move the right leg back. Let the right knee touch the ground and stretch the right foot backwards. Don't move the left foot or the hands. The left knee and foot should be vertically over each other.

5. Hold your breath and move the left leg back. Move the toes forward so the weight of the stretched legs rests on them. Hold the body, neck and head in a straight line. Do not move the hands.

6. As you exhale, bend your legs so the knees touch the ground. Do not move the feet. Let the chest and forehead touch the ground also. Do not move the hands. The elbows should not touch the ground and should touch the ribs. The bum will be raised.

7. As you inhale, point the toes backwards and arch backwards without moving the hands and keeping the elbows to the ribs.

8. As you exhale, without moving the hands, tuck your toes and raise the bum up high. Keep the spine and neck straight. If you can't keep your heels in the ground, it is okay to lift them a little.

9. As you inhale, move the right foot forward and place it between the hands. Drop the left knee to the ground and point the toes of the left foot backwards. Alternatively drop the left knee first, then move the right foot forward.

10. As you exhale, move the left foot forward next to the right foot. Stretch the legs. This posture is the same as the one in 3.

11. As you inhale, stand up straight and simultaneously move the arms in a circle in front of the body and above the body, then bend backwards and move the arms backwards as well. This posture is the same as in 2.

12. As you exhale stand up straight and bring the palms of the hands together in front of the chest. This posture is the same as in 1.

1-12 is one round. Do a few rounds, then lie down and rest a few minutes. Every other round you alternate the front and back leg in 4 and 9.

SELF-STUDY

It is very important that the student studies himself honestly and lovingly-critically; not just his personality, but also his beliefs and convictions. Anything the student is particularly fond of should be scrutinized. He should look for anything he clings to, holds onto or in any way is attached to or repulsed by. Once such has been found, the student should practice letting go of it. One aid in this is to witness it: You step out of the mind-involvement and rest in the empty silence in which the mind floats, so to speak. From that stance, observe the mind and the conviction it harbors. This helps develop detachment from the conviction. It is difficult to change a conviction one is attached to, so by developing detachment this way, it becomes easier to either change the conviction or get rid of it entirely.

Psychoanalysis is of course an efficient way of studying yourself, but it takes a lot of time, which could generally be better spent in meditation. A few psychotherapies also aid self-study and self-improvement, unless they are merely cathartic. Psychotherapies in general make people more self-willed, egocentric and even a bit bitchy. In other words, there is not much spirituality to be gotten from psychotherapy.

The best way to advance in self-study is to practice objectifying the subject. This involves stepping out of the mind and emotions and into the silent stance from where one can observe the thoughts and the emotions unaffected. The art is to practice it enough so that one does not get caught up in the emotions again once one begins to scrutinize them. With practice one can silently and unattached observe even strong emotions and turbulent thoughts without getting caught up in them. The next step is to scrutinize them objectively and disinterestedly. One should ask: Why is this feeling in my psyche? It is not me, what is my mind doing? Is it placing guilt onto others? Is it projecting? Is it being over-defensive? One should read about the psychological defense mechanisms (see the chapter at the end of this book) to become really good at asking such questions, because that will give one enough insight into the mind to ask pertinent questions and not just fumble around in the dark. Once one has spotted an unhealthy mechanism in the psyche, one should try to loosen it up. It helps a lot just to recognize it for what it is. But often there are underlying issues that also need to be recognized and lovingly released. Again, simply recognizing them helps a lot. We will look into the various psychological defense mechanisms in a later chapter.

THEORY

THE DARK NIGHTS

On the path to enlightenment people usually go through two dark nights, or periods of hardship. The first is of the mind, the second is of the soul. In the dark night of the mind you get rid of your beliefs. In the dark night of the soul you get rid of the believer.

Dark night of the mind

As you progress in meditation and begin to have some experiences of the Self, you begin to realize that your concepts about enlightenment are wrong. This night can also begin if you trust your teacher and challenge your own ideas about enlightenment based on his teachings. It goes deeper than just changing your mind since many of these core beliefs constitute the foundation of your sādhana and spiritual life. As these beliefs crumble, you may feel disillusioned and lose faith or want to give up sādhana altogether. But do not give up! Realize that your mind understands nothing and that it never can understand anything correctly about enlightenment. It makes you humble and this humility is a must on the spiritual path. If you cling to your ideas and refuse to give them up, it will be difficult to let go and merge into deep samādhi. If you happen to be a person with some authority in the spiritual community, all the worse since such authority will have to go along with the convictions it is based upon.

Dark night of the soul

As you experience the Self more and more you will gradually realize that you are not the small self, not the ego or the personality. You identify with these, but all such identifications will have to go and this is usually painful. It is like a sort of ego death. Saint John of the Cross, who wrote a book called The Dark Night (about 1578), later with 'of the Soul' added to the title, wrote that God takes those through the darkest night whom he wants to elevate to the greatest heights, and there is much truth to that. The greater the transparency of the ego and personality, the more the light of the Self, the Shakti, can shine through and manifest in the world around you. Dying to the personality has many effects. You might be proud of a particular part of the personality, some talent perhaps around which identity has formed; when this identification begins to go away the pride resists fiercely, and when it finally dies, you (as small self) feel lost and worthless for a while. Thus, through attrition, the ego-structures which hinder you from reaching higher states of enlightenment, gradually and painfully diminish.

THE PEARLS

Siddha yogis may see what we call 'pearls'. They are small, shimmering dots of light that appear in or out of meditation. There is a red, a white, a black and a blue pearl. The red, white and black belong to more and more subtle bodies. The red pearl is associated with the physical body. The white pearl with the astral body. The black pearl with the causal body. The blue pearl is completely transcendental and associated with the supracausal level of the absolute Self.

The blue pearl

Seeing the blue pearl is very auspicious; it indicates that there is established a connection within you to the Divine level of existence, even beyond the void realized in Self-realization. When you see the blue pearl, usually nothing happens beyond that. You do not spontaneously get blissful or elated. You just see this shimmering dot of cyan light. Take it as an inspiration, as an encouragement.

The blue pearl may pull you into it, and if that happens, you will find yourself in an infinite luminous cyan-colored space of pure consciousness, of pure being on a divine level. This *chit-akasha* (space or void of pure consciousness) is the source of everything. It permeates everything. It is pure bliss in the extreme. This is the abode of the Supreme Being. If you are lucky enough to be sucked into this space, you may also be lucky enough to have the darshan of the Supreme Being. This is extremely rare, though.

Map of Enlightenment

Awakening

This is not enlightenment, though many think it is. It is just a total reorientation of values and perspectives away from illusion. You now navigate towards the Absolute, rather than just being totally identified with the ego-mind-heart complex that is not you, but that you hitherto thought was you. You realize you are not the person, but that the person is something transient like the body, and that you essentially are void. There is a certain freedom in this, and many delude themselves that this is enlightenment. It is very far from enlightenment. People at this stage intuit the unmanifest and understand that since they are not something, they must be nothing, and just as they are nothing, everything else must be nothing, and they call this insight non-duality. However, even though what they say superficially sounds like Unity Consciousness, it is not. It is very easy to speak non-duality-talk. At this stage, you have fully realized you are not anything of the relative, but you have not – I repeat – you have not merged into the ultimate Void. You have realized you are not something, hence you must be nothing, but you have not merged into full realization of that nothingness.

Transcendental Consciousness

After Awakening and with diligent meditation, you may begin to get short bursts of oneness with the Self. With practice, they become longer and longer. This direct experience of the Self of course changes one's consciousness into another level, which can be called Transcendental Consciousness since one has become aware of the Self (which at this point is experienced as being transcendental).

I AM

As Transcendental Consciousness becomes habitual, you become established in the second most subtle state of ignorance: the I AM. This is still not enlightenment. Many people delude themselves at this point that they have become enlightened; that their person somehow has expanded or evolved to a higher state of being. Oh, so wrong! They think: '*I* am enlightened!' It is total nonsense and such grandiose narcissistic notions should be given up as soon as possible.

After giving up I AM you have to surrender the basic 'I-ness' or 'Individuation Principle' that comes prior to I AM and is the first point of ignorance. This point can rightly be called *bindu*, since it is like an infinitely small dot. Once you dissolve this back into void, you become Self-realized.

Self-realization

With diligent meditation after I AM, you may eventually merge into oneness with the Self that is so complete, that there is no returning back. This no returning back comes from the basic I-ness, or Individuation Principle, bindu, being utterly reabsorbed into the Self. Thus, ignorance is utterly destroyed and you are a Jīvan Mukta; A liberated soul. This is the first level of enlightenment. It is not bliss. Bliss comes later. In fact, in its purity, this state is just void.

In Self-realization, you are Shiva (as Pure Being) and this realization is irreversible and persistent throughout the other stages of enlightenment.

Having realized Shiva within, you now have to realize not only Shiva without, but also Shakti within and without. In other words, to progress further you have to awaken kundalinī.

When kundalinī awakens, it won't necessarily rise right away. You may feel heat in the spine and pressure in the brain as the crown chakra begins to open. Bliss states will grab you in meditation. The interesting thing is that if kundalinī awakens before Self-realization, you will get these raptures and bliss-states before Self-realization. On the other hand, if kundalinī is not awakened before Self-realization, you may think Self-realization is the end of the journey. The (wrong) logic being that there can be nothing higher than the unmanifest and you have realized the unmanifest.

However, you have only realized the unmanifest within. Now you need to realize it without.

God Consciousness (Lovebliss)

In this phase, you are somewhat mad. You are so madly in love with God and full of devotion, you cry for years (not constantly of course) and still your tears do not run dry. You begin to sense Mother Shakti in everything and perceive this as sensing God (in whatever form you like) in everything. It is an extremely blissful phase that may last several years in which you find God permeates everything, including you and your body. Every cell of the body vibrates with bliss (lovebliss). God Consciousness is not a stable state in itself, as Self-realization and Sahaja Samadhi are. Those two come with irreversible shifts in consciousness. God Consciousness is more a bridge between the two.

As time goes and you merge more and more with the bliss, Shakti begins to long for Shiva, so to speak. The next phase is a fusion of Shakti and Shiva. The bliss then diminishes and you may wonder if you have lost everything you had hitherto reached spiritually, but you have not, you are just moving beyond. The bliss will eventually return in a deeper and stronger way.

Unity Consciousness

Eventually the silvery kundalinī 'snake' leaves its resting place just above the perineum, enters the spine, moves up inside the spine and dissolves into blazing white light filling the spine, and finally merges back into the void (Shiva) in the brain. It is beyond outrageously blissful. Way beyond the bliss of God Consciousness, which in itself is way beyond the bliss ordinary people experience in moments of rapture or sex.

Eventually, as Shakti merges back into Shiva, you realize you are Shiva-Shakti and that everything is Shiva-Shakti. You perceive this unity in you and in everything around you. This is Unity Consciousness. You see the Self in everything.

When kundalinī completely merges with Shiva in the brain, the crown chakra opens completely. The crown chakra is then a ball of energy: a full sphere. Before that, it opens as a hemisphere covering the scull. Before that, it opens as a more or less five centimeter large disk or hole at the top of the scull.

Many people feel 'oneness with everything', especially nature, and think this is Unity Consciousness. It is not. It is just a mood of belonging to a holographically conceived universe, and it completely belongs to the mind. Delving in such is a waste of time. No ego can ever enter oneness with anything.

Unity Consciousness goes up and down in clarity. Sometimes you do not sense the Self in everything, yet you are of course completely aware of this oneness with nothing and of lovebliss inside (oneness is not the right word, because it implies multiplicity fused into one. Such multiplicity is false, but language presses us to express ourselves in terms of multiplicity). At other times, you are totally one with everything (again 'everything' is a term borrowed from the multiplicity-paradigm. There is no 'everything' since it is all Shiva-Shakti!

There is no You anymore and only Shiva-Shakti, or IT, and the sense that everything is lovebliss/the Self. These are extremes, of course; usually you have some medium state going up and down in clarity.

Sahaja Samādhi

As time goes by the fluctuations of Unity Consciousness flatten out and you enter a stable state of Unity. Sahaja samādhi does not have new qualities from Unity Consciousness. It is just that it becomes a completely stable state of constant awareness in your everyday life. 'Sahaja' means 'natural.' There is a certain change in that while you earlier had a sense that the bliss exploded in you, it now implodes. These are poor metaphors, of course. Language fails to describe this. Sahaja samādhi comes with a sudden shift, like Self-realization does. God consciousness and unity consciousness are more like phases; one gliding imperceptibly into the other.

Becoming a True Siddha

If the above states are rare, this is extremely rare. It can only be reached through Siddha Yoga, which means the Yoga of Shaktipāt. In this yoga, you get visions of what we call pearls: small luminous dots appearing in your field of vision whether your eyes are closed or open or whether you are meditating or not. In the beginning, they come in meditation, but later also when out of meditation. There is a white, a black, a red and a blue pearl. The Blue Pearl is the highest and seeing it is actually a blessing in itself, even though you may feel no different from seeing it. If you are fortunate enough to enter the Blue Pearl, you enter an infinite cyan-blue space, or infinite void of supreme cyan-blue lovebliss. It fills the entire universe, yet the entire universe is contained in that small pearl. If you have this supreme experience, or reach this state (language fails: you ARE THIS), which is the most supreme any yogi can have, then you by definition become a Siddha: A perfected being. The term 'Siddha' refers to a person who has been in (merged with) this Blue Infinity, at least temporarily. A Mahāsiddha has, at least temporarily merged with the Blue Being.

Other systems and schools use the word 'Siddha' differently, so don't think that just because someone calls himself or herself a Siddha, it means they have had this 'experience'. Usually it just means they are students of a so-called 'Siddha lineage' and may or may not have become enlightened in that lineage.

Meeting the Blue Being

Once inside the Blue Pearl and immersed in (merged with) the Blue Infinite Void, you may get the darshan of the Blue Being. He may appear as Lord Shiva or Krishna, or whom so-ever you are devoted to, or whom so-ever He chooses. All gods like Rama and Krishna and so on are avatars of this one Blue Being, who is the one God taking a personal form for the sake of His devotees. If you get His darshan, or better: if He makes you One with Him for a few moments, your full enlightenment is guaranteed and you will reach Shiva Consciousness eventually; if not in this life, then when you leave the body at death or in the next life if you choose to come back and continue your sādhana and help others.

Shiva Consciousness

If you enter the Blue Pearl and the pearl explodes so that you become permanently One with this Blue Infinite Void, then you become established in Shiva Consciousness. Or rather become Shiva Consciousness. You do not yet merge with the Blue Being. I am not in this state, though I have experienced it clearly enough, so I will refrain from further comments.

NĀDIS

Sushumnā

There are many thousands of energy channels (*nādis*) in the human body. Of these, by far the most important is *Sushumnā* inside the spine. The spinal column forms a tube and inside this tube you have the spinal cord which coincides with the Sushumnā nādi. Below you have a cross section of the spinal cord.

Within Sushumnā there is another nādi called *Vajra nādi* and it coincides with the white matter (1). Within Vajra there is a nādi 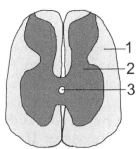 called *Chitra nādi* and it coincides with the grey matter (2). Within Chitra nādi there is another nādi called *Brahma nādi* and this coincides with *canalis centralis* (3) which is a hollow tube passing up through the center of the entire spinal column and into the brain where it merges into the ventricles (hollow cavities inside the brain) of the two hemispheres. The awakened kundalinī rises up inside Brahma nādi/canalis centralis and pours into the brain via the ventricles. Though kundalinī technically rises there, we normally just speak of kundalinī rising inside the Sushumnā/inside the spine.

Idā and Pingalā

Two other nādis are important: Idā and Pingalā. Idā starts from the right testicle/ovary and Pingalā from the left. Idā terminates at the left nostril, Pingalā at the right (as experienced from the person himself). What happens in-between is of some debate. Some say they run up on either side of the entire spine, some say they cross sides at every chakra, some say that they cross sides at each of the granthis. Idā is cooling and Pingalā is heating. Prāṇāyāmas utilize the energy flowing in Idā and Pingalā to open up the root of Sushumnā so that kundalini shakti will begin to flow there.

Amrita nādi

There is an energy channel running from the top of the head down the front of the body to the heart.

The frontal channel

There is a nādi running from the perineum to the top of the head along the front of the body. Some attempt to raise kundalinī up this channel, but that is a bad idea. Kundalinī belongs in the spine.

THE CHAKRAS

The chakras are metaphysical energy nexuses and centers with many functions. They are points where the soul interacts with the physical body and its existence in the world. They also channel vital force to the body. Certain psychological functions and qualities are also associated with them. There is really no reason to go into all these qualities, how many petals each chakra has, and so on. It is only important to have some knowledge of their existence and location, since kundalinī has to pierce them all in its journey to the brain. The chakras are located inside the Sushumnā, but they project out to the surface of the body, usually the front, and resemble flowers or wheels. These outward projections are called *kshetrams*, but many think of them as the chakras. (See next page).

Chakra	Location	Kshetram
7. Sahasrāra	Cerebrum	Top of the head
6. Ājnā	Pineal gland or Medulla Oblongata	Between the eyebrows
5. Vishuddhi	Behind the throat	Pit of throat
4. Anāhata	Between the shoulder blades	Center of chest
3. Manipura	Behind the solar plexus	Solar plexus
2. Swādhistāna	Between 1st lumbar vertebrae and sacrum	Between the pubic bone and the navel
1. Mulādhāra	Perineum	Perineum

During meditation one may see colors in the locations of the chakras. There are various opinions about the colors. The New Agers have had much success in promoting a set of colors that has little to do with the traditional colors. The New Age logic is that there are seven chakras and there are seven colors in the rainbow, so they should correlate. In their system, which was probably created in the 1980s, the chakras from the bottom-up are; red, orange, yellow, green, blue, indigo and violet. It is odd that the New Agers took the ancient Tantric concept of the chakras, but did not follow the ancient Tantric chakra colors. These are given in the following table. The crown chakra, sahasrāra, is so transcendental it does not have any color, or, when sensed in meditation, is blazing bright and multicolored like mother-of-pearl combined with gold.

Chakra	Mantra	Shakti mantra	Color	Color of element
Sahasrāra	Aum	Sauh or Saum		
Ājnā	Om	Haum	Transparent or grey	Transparent or grey
Vishuddhi	Ham	Kreem	Purple	Blue or white
Anāhata	Yam	Gaum	Blue	Light grey or smoky
Manipura	Ram	Aim	Yellow	Red
Swādhistāna	Vam	Hreem	Orange	White
Mulādhāra	Lam	Shreem	Red	Yellow

The chakras are located within the Brahma nādi and they do sometimes form impediments to kundalinī's ascension, but the properly awakened kundalinī shakti knows how to cleanse and open the chakras so it can ascend properly. It is a common misunderstanding that as kundalinī rises it opens the chakras one at a time from the bottom up. This is, emphatically, not the case. For some kundalinī goes straight to the Sahasrāra and grants the aspirant bliss directly after shaktipāt, after which kundalinī later, without diminishing the bliss or leaving the Sahasrāra in any major way, opens the other chakras (and not in a linear order from the top down, or bottom-up, or in any other given order). It is highly individual in which order the chakras open after shaktipāt and it is not good to assume that if it was like one order for somebody else, it should be like this for oneself also, or for everybody else.

When the yogi penetrates the Sahasrāra he enters the great void of the Absolute and realizes it as bliss and his very Self.

Other chakras

There are many more chakras than the seven mentioned above, which are considered the most important ones. Kashmir Shaivism, which flourished around the 11th century BC, worked with twelve:

12. Above the head (Bhramara chakra)
11. Sahasrāra
10. At the forehead (Purna-giri-pitha chakra)
9. Ājnā
8. At the nose (Balavat chakra)
7. Vishuddhi
6. Anāhata
5. Manipura
4. At the center of the navel (Manas chakra)
3. At the womb (Kundalinī chakra)
2. Swādhistāna
1. At the anus (Adhara chakra)

A note on clairvoyance and psychic abilities

When a chakra opens, it can sometimes bestow psychic abilities, like clairvoyance. Such powers, when arising, should generally be ignored and killed off. Some are born with the gift, of course, in which case it is part of their prārabdha karma, but this is rare. People who pursue developing clairvoyance are on a wrong path that will not lead to enlightenment and most certainly will impede it. One example is the clairvoyant ability to see other people's past lives. It is associated with Manipura, not the third eye as many believe, thus it is not a particularly high ability or indicative of spiritual advancement. That is why all such abilities are best left alone if they show up as you progress. Indulging in them will hold you back. Usually clairvoyants are just projecting their own subconscious into their 'channeled' messages anyway. They are all on an ego-trip. Just avoid them and avoid any such abilities that may arise in you. They are useless beyond ego-gratification. As you progress after Self-realization, some clairvoyant abilities will either remain or emerge, such as seeing where people are spiritually and being able to guide them, but these abilities will be kept secret.

THE THREE KNOTS (GRANTHIS)

There are three major blockages (granthis) for kundalinī's ascent from the root to the brain up through Sushumnā. Note that though these knots are associated with a chakra location, the granthis and the chakras are independent. Opening the heart chakra, for example, will not automatically untie the granthi at that location (Vishnu granthi).

Rudra granthi

At the top of the spine: At the Atlas bone where the spine meets the scull and into Medulla Oblongata. If you do not untie this knot, the shakti will not enter the brain but may flow along the outside of the scull instead. This can be quite pleasurable, but do not mistake it for the real bliss of the Self or assume it has anything to do with the crown chakra opening. Once this knot it untied and kundalinī shakti flows into the brain, then one has a good chance of getting enlightened in this lifetime. Love at this level is not an emotion; it is non-dual, without attachments and simply realized as the nature of one's Self.

Vishnu granthi

At the heart chakra. Almost no people can imagine above this level, hence they think of interpersonal love as the highest. They have no inkling of divine love or the love which is the Self. For them love is inseparable from desire and the bargain of mutual sensual gratification. True, most do feel love for the other person beyond gratification, simply because they like them, but what if that other person stops satisfying their desires, then their love would probably dwindle. The love that fills one when one opens

Vishnu granthi does not depend on this mutual exchange. One simply loves, yet the love is always dualistic. Below the heart, love always involves a bargain, a contract of some sort, though this of course is never formulated and probably not even conscious for most people. Even in cases where gratification ends, there can be other contracts at work, like sexual roles, security, being parents together, and so on. The love of the heart does not involve such contracts at all; love is simply there. This love, however, is still an emotion, a feeling; you as an individual subject feel love for an object, be it another person, an animal or whatever. This is dualistic love and it involves much attachment to the loved object.

Brahma granthi

At the root chakra. This knot blocks kundalinī's entrance into Sushumnā and thus kundalinī's possible arousal. This block is usually untied by the guru during shaktipāt initiation, at least to a large degree. Most people have this knot closed tight. This means they do not live beyond material safety, procreation, sensual pleasures and material acquisitions. Their spiritual progress will be very small, if at all. Love, for these people, cannot go beyond the tender care for the family. They confuse sexual desire with love and think sex makes love. Most contemporary western so called Tantra practitioners belong to this unevolved class, thus they speak of sexual intercourse as 'practicing Tantra'. Such nonsense!

Celibacy and Brahma granthi

Some yogis want to live in celibacy in order to transmute the sexual energy to spiritual energy. If they have not untied Brahma granthi, celibacy is not possible, or, if they manage to repress their sexuality, it will not be of any spiritual benefit, since the energy will not be able to sublimate and enter the Sushumnā.

KARMA

The word *karma* means 'action', but it specifically refers to the principle of cause and effect. Usually the word karma just refers to the effects or consequences of one's actions. Put simplistically, if you bang someone on the head, you will yourself later get banged on the head, if not in this lifetime, then in a future one. In this sense, if someone gets banged on the head, he might tell himself it was just bad karma and forgive whoever hit him. At best this leads to compassion, at worst it leads to apathy. The apathy sets in when people justify not doing anything about the problems of their current situation by saying it is just karma anyway (implying there is nothing to do about it). But karma comes to us to incite us to do something! This does not mean taking revenge, it means forgiving and moving on, or changing your circumstances to the better if they are unsatisfactory.

Three kinds of karma

Sanchita karma
This is the huge amount of karma you have accumulated over the many past lives you have lived. It is like a huge storehouse of dried seed. Not all of these seeds will sprout and come to fruition in the present life. Unless you destroy this store of karma, you are bound to many future lives. The best way to deal with Sanchita karma is to do sādhana and the best sādhana is of course shaktipāt sādhana since this involves the awakened kundalinī and this awakened kundalinī, so to speak, roasts the karmic seeds so they no longer can sprout.

Prarabdha karma
This is the small portion of the Sanchita karma that you have to live out in this life. There is no escaping it, no matter how enlightened you become. It is as if a bunch of arrows were fired at birth and they are flying through time and space to hit their respective targets at various times in your present life. The arrows are fired and you cannot stop them. You can, however, move from

the place the arrows will hit and thus diminish the effect of the karma. Sādhana is the best way to move your position, but the karma will still hit, though with less force.

Kriyāmana karma (and Agami karma)

This is karma that you are presently performing and creating. As you are reading this book, this act of reading is Kriyāmana karma. It is not the fruit of anything in particular, you are simply reading. Of course, there are deeper underlying reasons for reading this particular book at this particular time, but that is not a concern of the notion of Kriyāmana karma. It is simply what you are doing right now. Kriyāmana karma normally adds to the huge store of Sanchita karma. But whether this is the case and it creates future karma to be endured or not depends on many things. If you are enlightened and beyond the *gunas* (the three primal energies of creation), it will not create Sanchita karma. There is a fourth kind of karma, which is a subcategory of Kriyāmana karma: *Agami karma*. It is the karma that you are forced to perform due to other karmas you have performed in this life. There is no free will in this. For example, if your present action is to take a bath in the tub, you are bound to get out of the tub sometime in the future; that getting out is Agami karma. If you give all your money to the poor so you cannot pay your rent, then getting evicted is your Agami karma. Giving the money in itself may be good karma (for future lives), but you will get evicted nonetheless.

Giving up all karma (good or bad)

Karma in itself does not distinguish between good and bad; it just does what it is bound to do; like a spring that unwinds once it is released. From the point of view of getting enlightened, 'good' karma is just as useless as 'bad' karma. People call karma that has unpleasant results 'bad' – karma that has pleasant results 'good'. But there is no good or bad karma, there is just karma, and as far as getting enlightened is concerned it is all a trap. You have to step out of all karma. Of course, this does not justify creating bad karma, which you emphatically should avoid, but you should step out of the field of karma altogether.

FREE WILL

Do people have free will? Yes and no! Consider this: You are crossing the zebra crossing and a careless driver runs you down. You had no free will there; your bad karma just acted itself out. You have a business, but suddenly the market changes and you are ruined. No free will there, your bad karma just acted itself out. You are single, a suitable partner woos you; you can say yes or no. Here you have free will. You win the lottery; you can say yes or no to the money. Here you have free will. What we can conclude from this is that you have free will with respect to good karma, but not with respect to bad karma. Bad karma just hits you no matter what. You can protect yourself, take precautions, insure yourself and so on, but it hits nevertheless. The question that follows after this is: What made you decide like you did with respect to your good karma? What made you accept it, what reject it? This is exceedingly complex and beyond the scope of this book, but everyone can agree that your history of good and bad karma led you to choose as you did. This means that all along you have had at least free will regarding your choices about what to do with your good karma. It is worth noting that when someone created the bad karma, they had free will with respect to whether they would create the bad karma or not. This means that at the end of the argument you have free will as to whether you will relinquish your free will and surrender to the forces of bad karma at play in your life by creating more bad karma. The more bad karma, the less free will! The more good karma, the more free will! No matter what, when bad karma hits you, you have free will with respect to how you react. Some have more options, others less. This again depends on the balance between good and bad karma in the person's life. No one is ever without the choice of how to react to bad karma. Basically, you have two options: you can seek revenge or you can forgive. Seeking revenge creates more bad karma and reduces your free will. Forgiving creates good karma and enhances your free will.

Psychological Defense Mechanisms

There is a reason it is called 'defense' mechanisms. It could also be called defense 'strategies', which probably is more true to what actually goes on in the psyche. They are called 'defenses' because they are psychological reactions and behaviors that are intended to protect ourselves from pain. Defense mechanisms are not symptoms of a sick soul; they are natural strategies most people develop during infancy and early childhood because they are not mature enough to know of better ways of handling their anxiety, pain or frustration. Defense mechanisms do become problematic when adults resort to them over and over again. Defense mechanisms usually show themselves as unconscious reactions and more mature individuals can get quite surprised when they discover they spontaneously resorted to one of them. They are rarely rational. Recognizing the defenses as they control our behavior, and resolving them and developing more rational and mature reactions is an important part of psychological growth and maturity. Some are more primitive than others, which has led psychologists to group the defense mechanisms into three categories:

1. Primitive
These are inefficient in the long run, but can work in the immediate situation. They are developed during childhood and mostly found in children, but many adults never move beyond these primitive defenses. It takes a certain effort to move beyond primitive defenses and learn new strategies, and if a person is not mature enough to do the work required, he may resort to the primitive defenses all his life.

2. Less primitive, somewhat mature
These defenses are a step up from the primitive defenses and are more socially acceptable, though they do not do the person any good in the long run. Neurotic individuals rely heavily on them.

3. Mature

Mature defenses are the most useful for adults and they can be classified as quite healthy. Remember that everybody uses defenses and these mechanisms are part and parcel of how the psyche operates. The task for the individual who wants to mature psychologically is to move beyond the primitive and less primitive mechanisms to the mature mechanisms. They help the individual be a constructive element of society in the most positive sense of the expression.

Primitive defenses

Denial

This is self-explanatory. It is probably the most primitive of all the defense mechanisms. The person simply refuses to accept something and acts as if it does not exist. It can for example be an event, a fact, a thought or a feeling that is being denied. Even though it is so primitive one should expect people to recognize it at once, most people use it now and then when they have troubling emotions, inappropriate sexual urges, behaviors they are embarrassed about, and so on. Self-indulgence, for example, is often denied. People who abuse recreational drugs most likely deny they have a problem. We have all met the nicotine addict who denies that fact by saying he is merely a social smoker. Of course, when people are in denial, it is impossible to help them and they will have a hard time helping themselves.

Regression

This involves a reversion to an earlier stage of psychological development, to immature patterns of behavior. Counterproductive as this may sound, it is also common. Some examples: When faced with the prospect of a lover chucking you, a person may revert to an infantile stage and become clingy. Some adults, when overwhelmed with problems, just want to stay in bed all day. Or they expect their partner to pamper them as if they were a small child. Some throw temper tantrums, for example when they are stuck in a traffic jam or they miss a plane. People, who as a reaction to feeling mad drive recklessly or refuse to talk to people of course only make the situation worse.

Acting out

When a person is incapable of expressing his emotions or thoughts, he may resort to extreme behavior that dramatizes the inner tension. He could beat a pillow or bang a fist against the wall. Ashtrays may be thrown through the room or plates or cups of coffee or what not. A rational reaction in all these instances would be to simply say 'I am angry!' and try to solve whatever causes the anger. Acting out solves nothing, but it does give some a short term feeling of release. Acting out of course stems back to the infantile stage where the child throws a temper tantrum or breaks things by throwing them across the room. It has its value at that age, because the infant does not yet have strategies for solving his or her immediate problem. But it certainly has very little value in an adult.

Dissociation

This peculiar defense involves losing contact with what is actually going on and stepping into an alternative 'reality' where there are no emotional tensions, troubling thoughts or unpleasant memories or situations. Victims of child abuse often develop this radical defense mechanism. An extreme example is when a person develops a second personality and jumps into this personality when the natural personality becomes too painful to be in. The rare extreme of this is of course known as multiple personality disorder. But more normal people also dissociate when they find themselves in an unpleasant situation and pull up an alternative personality that can handle the situation. They can have a cold professional persona, for example, and a kind and loving persona, and jump between these whenever they find one gives more relief than the other. A person disposed to anger may dissociate from the angry personality and develop a sweet and mild persona that is completely out of contact with the anger; such a person may flip-flop between the two personas quite rapidly, much to the surprise of those close the him or her, and still the person may not realize that he or she has an anger problem.

Compartmentalization

This is a minor form of dissociation. Parts of the psyche are compartmentalized, meaning they are out of contact with each other. One part may be very honest and have great moral integrity, while the other part cheats on the income tax return. Because the person has compartmentalized the two parts of his psyche, he will not feel any incongruity or conflict. A girl might be controlling and moralizing over her partner about being faithful, while she herself is a notorious flirt.

Projection

Here a person ascribes his own unpleasant feelings, thoughts, ideas, urges, impulses and so on to someone else who does in fact not have any of those. In a marriage, for example, one of the partners may accuse the other of being unfaithful, when in fact it is he or she who is harboring desires for another person or is indeed unfaithful. Someone who is angry with another person may accuse the other person of being angry, even though that is not the case. Someone who is lying to his or her partner may accuse the partner of lying. Someone who has had a special hairdo and regrets it may feel her friends are laughing at her behind her back because of it, and even verbally and angrily accuse them of it, and so on. Projection is normally a result of lack of insight into one's own psyche and what is going on there. By mis-attributing unpleasant psychic material to someone else, the person can delude himself that he does not have those unpleasant feelings, motivations, and so on, and is actually a victim of them.

Reaction formation

This defense turns unpleasant emotions, thoughts, urges and so on into their opposite. We can, for example, see this in marriages where a person is married to someone who abuses them either physically or psychologically, and they instead of leaving the bad partner, cling to him or her and love them all the more. Someone who hates his job may tell the boss how happy he is with it and even convince himself he means it. An insecure person may act bossy or make displays of being confident. A boss might give an employee he is frustrated with a raise. We might also see positive emotions like love turned into aversion in the case of someone who is out of touch with his sexuality or uncomfortable with It. If someone woos him, he might think or speak badly about that person or feel angry with her instead of feeling positive, sympathetic emotions.

Less primitive defense mechanisms

Repression
This is normally a completely unconscious defense, so people usually have very little control over it. It involves blocking unpleasant urges, memories, etc. so they do not enter into consciousness. Someone may have unwanted memories, feelings or urges and push them out of awareness and into the subconscious. Defense mechanisms often cooperate with each other. A person who had an abusive father may have repressed those childhood memories and may furthermore use reaction formation to love the father and think of him as a decent, loving man.

Displacement
This ineffective defense mechanism involves having negative thoughts, feelings, and so on towards one person, but taking them out on another, who is less threatening. For example, a person may be angry with his boss, but can't say so for fear of being fired; he will then take his anger out on his wife when he gets home and start a fight. The wife then takes it out on the kid. The kid then takes it out on the dog. Of course, this defense mechanism is severely destructive, since it just ruins perfectly good relationships and creates further problems.

Intellectualization
This involves an overemphasis on thinking when confronted with an unpleasant situation, impulse, urge, and so on, instead of accepting it as it is and allowing a healthy emotional response to form. Intellectualization is a way of distancing oneself from unpleasant emotions, events and situations. For example,

someone's partner dies in an accident; the grieving person then avoids the pain by going into all the mental tasks of planning a funeral, taking care of the will, contacting the family, speculating about the accident and how it could have been avoided, and so on.

Rationalization

Rationalization is defined as: *Creating false but plausible excuses to justify unacceptable behavior*. For example, a shoplifter may justify his behavior with 'they can afford it'. Another type of rationalization could be this: Rather than feeling a healthy emotional response to a painful situation involving someone else, a person may try to stay on top by thinking, for example, 'I knew I could not trust him, he is mean' and stay with that seemingly 'superior' position rather than feel sad or hurt. Or person A loves person B and they are in a relationship; B suddenly dumps A; A then, instead of feeling sad, begins to find reasons why it is a good thing he is now free of B, why B was actually an unlovable jerk, and so on.

Undoing

If you hurt your spouse unintentionally by a careless remark, you might try to undo it by telling him or her how much you love them, how sweet and beautiful they are, buying flowers, and so on. All in the hope that by making amends it will balance the wrongdoing out. Some people, if they do something they regret, try to undo it by imposing on themselves something they must do to counteract what they regret having done.

Identification

Identification can be defined as: *Bolstering self-esteem by forming an imaginary or real alliance with some person or group.* Insecure people do this often, but anyone who joins a club, fraternity, sports team or a subculture, who follows a certain dress-code, hairstyle, and so on is subject to identification.

Mature defense mechanisms

Sublimation
Basically, this involves channeling psychic energy from one area to another. Unwanted impulses, emotions or thoughts may be defused by spending the energy involved on something else, like sports, art, music, and so on. It is not just sexuality that can be sublimated, of course, but anger, anxiety and other emotions too. Humor is another way of sublimating painful emotions or thoughts into a funny story or joke one can laugh at. Fantasizing can also be used to sublimate; if in a painful situation, some diffuse it by fantasizing about a better future.

Compensation
If a person has a weakness or deficiency in one area he or she may emphasize his or her talents in other areas in order to counterbalance the weakness, thus reinforcing the person's self-esteem. For example, someone may be terrible at math and may compensate by being verbally adept. A kid may be terrible at sports and may compensate by specializing in classical music, or vice versa.

Other forms of defense

Asceticism
The conscious denial of sensual pleasures with the aim of sublimating or repressing them entirely is a defense mechanism one now and then sees in spiritual people or lonely individuals. People who have chosen a quiet lifestyle of contemplation can use asceticism and sublimation with success. It is sadder when lonely people have given up finding happiness and resort to asceticism for solace.

Distortion

Under this heading we find grandiose delusions, wish-fulfilling delusions, hallucinations and other unrealistic ideas about the self, or others or the world for that matter. They usually serve to support delusional feelings of superiority or entitlement.

Blocking

This closely resembles repression, but here the individual feels tension when the impulse, emotion or thought is inhibited. Thinking can be blocked, like when people suddenly have an empty mind during a conversation that might have some unpleasant content for them

Hypocondriasis

For the purpose of evasion and regression, a person may exaggerate, overemphasize or conjure up an illness. A person reproaching himself for loneliness, bereavement, aggressive impulses towards others, and so on, can transform these unpleasant emotions into self-reproach and various bodily illnesses or physical pain. This way they can avoid taking responsibility for their negative impulses or painful emotions and feel sorry for themselves instead of reproachful.

Introjection

This involves internalizing the qualities of something or someone external. If a person is subject to aggressive behavior from someone, he or she may identify with the aggressor and try to be like him or her. Another example of introjection is when a person avoids the pain of separation from a loved one by absorbing and identifying with qualities of the loved one; such a loved one may be dead, but not necessarily. It can happen with a marriage partner as well, for example, or a friend.

Passive-aggressive

Here a person expresses aggressive emotions towards another by being passive or masochistic. Examples include procrastination, failure and illnesses or accidents that affect others more than oneself. By hurting themselves a little, they intend to hurt others more.

Appendix

DICTIONARY OF YOGIC TERMS

Absolute, the: In the context of yoga this refers to the innermost pure Being of a person. Since there is nothing beyond it and it is unmanifest, it is considered absolute.

Advaita: 'Non-duality'. It generally refers to the monistic philosophical systems of the Upanishads and Shankarāchārya, called Advaita Vedānta. But there are various non-dual schools in Indian philosophy. The basic tenet being that since the absolute Self is unmanifest there can be no duality in it. Anything that can be seen as within duality is rejected as false and as ignorance.

Amma: 'Mother'. The Divine mother. This nickname specifically refers to the contemporary saint Mata Amritānandamayi, also nicknamed 'The Hugging Saint'. Born Sept. 23, 1957 in Kerala, India.

Amrita: 'Immortality', 'ambrosia', 'Divine nectar'. 1. In deep meditation, one can sometimes sense a sweetish taste in the mouth, which is a release of amrita. It does not taste like anything else. 2. Metaphorically it refers to the intense bliss one experiences when merged with the absolute Self. 3. The absolute Self, which is immortal.

Ānanda: 'Supreme bliss'. Ānanda is one aspect of the nature of the absolute Self. It is not an emotion. Ānanda is not tranquil pleasure or worldly joy. It is a state that can be reached in deep meditation beyond ecstasy. Ecstasy itself lies beyond joy.

Ānandamoyi Ma: A highly enlightened female saint from Bengal, India. *April 30, 1896; †1982.

Āsana: 'Posture'. 1. Any one of a large body of well-defined postures used in Hatha yoga for purification and strengthening of the body. 2. The place where a yogi sits.

Avadhoota: 'Cast off'. 1. A yogi who has cast off all worldly things, concerns and bonds. 2. An enlightened yogi whose manners and behaviors do not conform to moral or ethical standards.

Bandha: 'Bond', 'lock'. 1. One of a well-defined set of methods that seek to stop or direct the flow of vital force (prāna) in the body by adopting certain localized positions or contractions. 2. The state of ignorance, being one of bondage to physical existence. 3. Binding the consciousness to a given object as a practice for concentration.

Bhakta: A yogi who follows the path of devotion to God, *bhakti*.

Bhakti: 'Devotion', 'love', specifically, devotion to God as a spiritual path, bhakti yoga. See *parabhakti*.

Bindu: 'Dot'. 1. A source point which is the origin of all manifestation. 2. An energetic point at the back of the scull.

Bliss: See ānanda.

Blue Being: The Supreme Being. Adi Purusha, God. This Supreme Being incarnates from time to time. One such incarnation was Krishna. In extremely deep meditation the yogi may be blessed by the Supreme Being with his *darshan*, in which case he appears within as a Being made of radiant blue light, which is inseparable from and one with pure absolute consciousness. Such a darshan is blissful in the extreme and transforms the yogi completely; it guarantees his full enlightenment. See *Blue Pearl*.

Blue Pearl: In or out of meditation, the Siddha yogi may sporadically see a small luminous cyan dot shimmering in his field of vision. The Blue Pearl is the gateway to the chit ākāsha (the 'space' of absolute, supreme consciousness) in which the *Blue Being* resides. In very deep meditation this blue pearl may suck the yogi in, so that he suddenly finds himself in the infinite luminous cyan chit ākāsha. This is extremely rare, though.

Brahmacharya: 'Brahmic conduct', 'following the path of Brahma'. 1. Celibacy. 2. Causing the shakti, that is normally wasted in sex and the functions of the sexual organs, to rise in the *Brahma nādi*.

Brahma nādi: The innermost subtle energy channel, *nādi*, within the spine in which the kundalinī rises when awakened. It is situated within the canalis centralis in the middle of the spinal column.

Chakra: 'Wheel'. One of a number of esoteric energy centers in the subtle body (bodies). The common model lists the seven well known chakras, but there are many more. Kashmir Shaivism, for example, operated with twelve.

Darshan: 'Vision'. Having the audience of, or a meeting with an enlightened person or the Supreme Being. One can also have the darshan of celestial beings, discarnated yogis, and so on.

Divine Mother: see Mother Divine.

Enlightenment: in yoga there are basically two levels of enlightenment: 1. Liberation from false notions of the real Self, of one's essential Being. 2. Realization of the Supreme Being.

Granthis: 'Knots'. In yogic lore, this specifically refers to three contractions within the Brahma nādi that impede kundalinī's rising to the brain. They are situated at the root chakra; at the heart chakra: and at the base of the scull, at the Atlas bone.

Guna: 'Quality'. In yogic lore, there are three gunas, which form the basic building blocks of nature: Sattva (brightness), rajas (activity) and tamas (inertia, dullness). Beyond the gunas lies the absolute Self, hence the yogi seeks to transcend the gunas.

Guru: Spiritual teacher. Etymologically 'gu' means 'darkness' and 'ru' means 'light that dispels darkness', hence the guru is the spiritual teacher who dispels the ignorance of the student and enlightens him.

Hatha yoga: A school of *yoga* that focuses on various disciplines for attaining enlightenment. These include *āsanas, prānāyāma*, withdrawal from sensual impressions, concentration, meditation and, finally, *samādhi*.

Intensive: A group event spread over several days, typically three or five, that specifically is about shaktipāt initiation. A retreat or workshop that is not about giving shaktipāt initiation, is not an intensive.

Kanda: 'Bulb'. The point of origin of all the *nādis*. It is situated about an inch above the perineum.

Karma: 'Action'. A force generated by one's thoughts, intentions and behavior which causes future events in one's life to happen. Karma in itself is neutral, neither good nor bad though it is common to divide karma like that.

Kirtans: Devotional call and response singing, where the singer sings devotional songs or chants and the audience responds either by repeating or with a set response.

Knots: see *Granthis*.

Krishna: 'Dark blue', 'puller'. One of several incarnations of the Supreme Being, the *Blue Being*; in this case known as Vishnu. He is called 'puller' because he pulls the hearts of his devotees. He is said to have been born on July 27, 3112 BC.

Kriyā: 'Act', 'rite'. 1. After kundalinī has been awakened and is transforming the system of the yogi, the yogi may experience spontaneous and somewhat involuntary movements of limbs, spontaneous talking (usually gibberish), spontaneous strong emotions, inner visions, etc.; all these are gathered under the heading 'kriyās'. 2. A specific action to be performed as part of a given sādhana. 3. 'Kriyā Yoga', a specific set of kriyās; there are several kriyā yoga schools that define various kriyās as part of the set.

Kshetram: 'Place'. The outer, larger, manifestation of the chakra, which is located on the surface of the body. The root chakra kshetram is at the perineum; the crown chakra kshetram is at the top of the scull; the others are at the front of the body.

Kundalinī: 'coiled one'. The primal contraction of the unmanifest Shakti of the absolute Self. As kundalinī finishes manifesting the individual person, it coils up, in a snake-like form, three and a half times at the root chakra and goes to 'sleep'. The metaphor 'sleeping' kundalinī, means that the kundalinī continues to function as the primal energy in man, but does not much further his spiritual progress.

Kundalinī process: Once kundalinī has been awakened it will ceaselessly work for the liberation and full enlightenment of the yogi. This operation is termed 'the kundalinī process'. Taking it to the end means kundalinī has granted the yogi full enlightenment and has finally merged back into Shiva (The void of the unmanifest absolute Self); this does not mean the yogi dies, since shakti continues to operate in his system in an unrestricted form. Such a yogi no longer has a kundalinī 'snake', but is a living embodiment of Shakti.

Liberation: See *Mukti*.

Mālā: A rosary of beads or seeds. Usually such mālās have 108 or 54 beads, plus one. The seeds are typically *Rudraksha*.

Mantra: a syllable (a bija mantra) or a short or longer phrase that one mentally repeats, or remembers, as a means of meditation. Examples of bija mantras could be 'aim', 'hrim', 'klim'. Longer mantras could be 'Om Namah Shivayah' or 'Om Klim Parashaktiyai Namaha'.

Mooladhāra: The root chakra at the perineum.

Mother Divine: Adishakti, Parashakti. 1. The supreme deity as source of everything that has life, consciousness and power. 2. Shakti personified as Devi (also known as Mahādevi). 3. Shakti personified as Durga, the slayer of evil; and as Kālī (also called Chamunda), destroyer of demons and ignorance. For this reason, Kālī is often a favorite of yogis. 4. She has several manifestations as wives of various Hindu gods: Pārvatī, wife of Shiva; Lakshmī, wife of Vishnu; Saraswatī, wife of Brahma.

Mudrā: 'Seal'. A psychic attitude usually associated with a physical counterpart, like focusing the eyes at the third eye or the nose tip, intended to control the flow of vital force (prana). See *Bandha*.

Mukti: (Moksha) 'Liberation'. Liberation occurs when the conscious self-awareness merges back into the unmanifest, absolute Self and nothing relative remains. One is liberated from ignorance about the Self as well as from involuntary reincarnations forced upon one by karma.

Non-duality: See *Advaita*.

Parabhakti: The supreme devotion that arises in an enlightened yogi who has realized first the impersonal void, then realizes that the ultimate reality is not impersonal, but suprapersonal. Before Self-realization, parabhakti is not possible. Parabhakti begins when the Self-realized yogi begins to move forward from the non-dual void and realizes the existence of the Supreme Being (adi-purusha) and approaches this supreme being through parabhakti.

Paramguru: 1. The guru of the current guru. 2. The original guru who instigated a given lineage.

Patanjali: The sage who formalized yoga in his famous text, Yoga-Sūtras. Lived approximately 400 BC.

Prānāyāma: 'Breath control'. Any one out of a body of well-defined breathing patterns and breath controls used as a method in sādhana. In general they seek to channel the vital force, prāna, into the Sushumnā.

Prarabdha karma: The *karma* that one has decided to live out in the given incarnation.

Rajas: See *Gunas*.

Rāma: Like *Krishna* an avatar of the Supreme Being, in Hinduism known as Vishnu. The time of his life fades into the uncertain.

Rāmakrishna: A highly enlightened saint of Bengal, India. *February 18, 1836; †1886.

Ramana Maharshi: A highly enlightened sage, considered the father of modern non-duality teachings. *December 30, 1879; †1950.

Ramanuja: The sage who founded the school of Vedānta known as 'Vishishtadvaita', meaning 'modified nonduality'. He stressed the importance of *bhakti* and also that though the individual absolute Selves are unmanifest, they remain individual. This conflicts with *Advaita* Vedānta, which teaches there is only One unmanifest Self, called Brahman. *1017; †1137.

Rudraksha: 'Rudra's (Shiva's) teardrops'. These are seeds of the rudraksha tree. When dried they are used to make rosaries (*mālās*) and pendants. Rudraksha seeds can hold spiritual energy, shakti, to a high degree, hence yogis like to wear them.

Sādhana: 'Means of accomplishment'. A set of various disciplines practiced or followed with the aim of reaching enlightenment.

Samādhi: A temporary state of introspection in which one is more or less united with the absolute Self. There are numerous levels and variations of samādhi. In general, they designate an internal state beyond meditation. In the highest samādhi, one has left all false sense of self behind and merged into oneness with the Supreme Self.

Sangha: 'Community'. This is actually a Buddhist term, but it is in widespread use to designate the community of students around a guru, including the guru.

Sat-Chit-Ānanda: 'Being-concsiousness-bliss'. This phrase is an attempt to describe the nature of the absolute Self. They are not qualities, or distinguishable, but the essence of the Self as One. 'Consciousness' is not used in the traditional Western sense of being aware of something, but refers to the potential for such awareness; also, it refers to the fact that the absolute Self is self-aware. 'Bliss', *ānanda*, is not to be confused with an emotion or mood; nor is it ecstasy.

Sattva: See *gunas*.

Shakti: 'Power', 'The able One'. See *Mother Divine*.

Shaktipāt: 'Descent of Shakti'. The initiation by which an enlightened Siddha guru awakens the kundalinī in the aspirant. It can also be given by the Divine. It is considered an act of grace and not something the aspirant can make happen.

Shankarāchārya: (Shankara). The sage who revived Upanishadic *Advaita* Vedānta. *788 CE; †820.

Shiva: 'The auspicious one'. 1. The eternally in itself abiding nature of the absolute Self. Pure Being. 2. One of the principal Gods of Hinduism, where He is seen as the transformer (Brahma is the creator and Vishnu the upholder). In the Shakti traditions, Mother is seen as the principal deity and Shiva as secondary. In the Shiva traditions this is reversed, also here Shiva is seen as the creator, protector and transformer of the universe.

Siddha: 'Perfected One'. An enlightened master within a Siddha tradition. Siddha traditions usually rely on shaktipāt initiation, but not necessarily.

Surya Namaskara: 'Salutations to the sun'. A series of twelve āsanas adopted in succession in tune with the in- and out-breath. Various traditions include different āsanas in the series.

Sushumnā: 'Most gracious'. This is the major nādi (subtle energy-channel) inside the spinal column through which the awakened kundalinī rises to the brain.

Swādhistāna: The second chakra. Placed just above the sacral bone.

Tamas: See *Gunas*.

Tantra: (Tantrism). The spiritual school based on the ancient texts called Tantras. Its history is obscure. Contemporary so called 'Tantra' has turned Tantra into a sexual circus, but that is not what Tantra really or traditionally is about. Out of the about 200 Hindu Tantric texts that are extant, only one in passing mentions coitus as one of many possible pleasures in life. Buddhist Tantra, as distinguished from Hindu Tantra, seems to be more sexually oriented.

Yoga: 'Union'. Tradition of spiritual discipline aimed at taking the *yogi* to union with the absolute Self. Yoga was first compiled into a manual by *Patanjali* in his famous *Yoga Sūtras*. Today there are many branches of yoga.

Yoga Sūtras: Patanjali's famous manual on yoga, which was the first systematic compilation of yogic lore. From about 400 BC.

Yogi: A practitioner of yoga dedicated to reaching Self-realization.

Links

Requests for shaktipāt in absentia initiation:

Jan Esmann: jan@lovebliss.eu

Calendar of shaktipāt intensives:

www.lovebliss.eu/events-calendar.html

or:

www.shaktipat.eu

THE AUTHOR

Jan Esmann, M.A., B.A., B.Sc.. Born January 18, 1960, 8:35 PM, Copenhagen, where he still lives and works.

Jan has meditated since being a young teenager. He has an MA in the History of Modern Culture, a B.A. in Rhetorics and a B.A. in Literary Theory, all from Copenhagen University, also a B.Sc. From The Royal Academy of Arts, Copenhagen. He is a professional artist (www.janesmann.com) and has a software company (www.powerretouche.com), as well as being a member of MENSA and former member of ISPE (International Society of Philosophical Enquiry).

Other books by Jan Esmann

On spirituality:
Lovebliss – the Essence of Self-realization
Enlightenment 101 – From Ignorance to Grace
Kundalini Tantra – Song of Liberation
On the materials and methods of the artist:
The Artist's Craft – A Handbook.
On art history:
Figurative Art of the 21st Century
Short stories (in Danish)
Strandvaskeren

Contributions
Preface to Lynette Rogers: Sacred Mandala: lives touched by David Spero's transmission teaching, USA, 2016.

Articles (in Danish)
Modernismens astrallegeme – in: *Kritik* 143, Copenhagen, Denmark.
Jamen, det ligner jo noget – feature article in *Information* Sept. 23, 2000, Copenhagen.
...men er det kunst? - feature article in *Information* Dec. 2, 2000, Copenhagen.
Gud lader sig erfare, feature article in *Berlingske Tidende*, Aug. 8, 1998. Copenhagen.
Dr. Caligaris Kabinet rekonstrueret - eller dekonstruktion anno 1919, in *K&K* 81, 1996, Copenhagen.
Cyberpsykose, feature article about violence in computer games, in: *Politiken* Jan. 1 1995, Copenhagen
Cyberpsykose – a debate about violence in computer games and media between Jan Esmann and Carsten Jessen in: *Tidsskrift for Børne og Ungdomskultur*, 35, 1995, Denmark.
Debat om Rudolf Steiner (*Weekendavisen* gennem april og maj 1995)
Steiner-impulsen - en kritisk præsentation af Steiners Lære, Antroposofi, i *Dialog* 61 og 62, 1995, Århus.
Rabbinsk tænkning, mystik, psykokabbalisme og postmoderne tekstteori in: *K&K* 78, 1995. Copenhagen.
Sort i sort - da Gud reinkarnerede i modernismen in *Kritik* 119, 1995. Copenhagen.
Omkring et billede - analyse af et maleri af Rousseau. In *Kritik*, June 1994, Copenhagen.
På sporet af billedets semantik in *Litteratur & Samfund* 1988, Copenhagen.

Books about Jan Esmann
Bente Hammershøy: Jan Esmann – Paintings and Drawings, Copenhagen, 2016.